A
LIFE SHORT
& LOUD
AND THE LONG ROAD BACK

KEVIN W. LUBY

SMILE

Music by Charles Chaplin Words by John Turner and Geoffrey Parsons
© Copyright 1954 by Bourne Co.
Copyright Renewed
All Rights Reserved International Copyright Secured
ASCAP

I JUST GO

Music and Words by Boz Scaggs
© Copyright 2001 by William R. Scaggs & Dominique G. Scaggs, co-trustees of the
W&D Scaggs Revocable Trust u/a/d May 21, 1998 (d.b.a. Windover Lake Songs)
All Rights Reserved International Copyright Secured
ASCAP

ISBN-13: 978-1501045493
ISBN-10: 1501045490

table of contents

dedication

This book is dedicated, first and foremost, to my family—Jane, Conner, and Moira. You have made me who I am which, as it turns out, is much more than I thought was possible and likely more than I deserve.

I owe a great debt to a number of people who have helped me with this book. Thanks to my good friend Ken Cruickshank for constantly encouraging me (and occasionally hectoring me) and making me believe that I really could write a book. Thanks to my amateur editors, Cate Daraee, Alan Howard, Bob Thurber, and Pete Metropulos, as well as my professional editor, Mary Rosenblum.

I can't help but acknowledge that this book would be a grammatical nightmare if not for the herculean efforts of Angela Groce and Megan Jones née McAninch.

Thanks to Mike Kelley for repeatedly reminding me that I had a story to tell. As to everyone else who contributed to this book or who encouraged me to write it, you have my eternal gratitude.

A special thanks to Lisa Dillon of Lisa Dillon Photography for the cover photograph and Kelly Mooney of Kelly Mooney Photography for the picture of me.

If this turns out to be nothing more than a cathartic exercise for me, it will be well worth it. I hope, however, that this book will provide some consolation and succor to those who have suffered, or who may in the future suffer, a loss similar to our loss of Conner.

Finally, thanks to anyone and everyone who was kind to my family.

chapter one
the call

"Daddy, the police are here. Conner's dead."

chapter two
the boy

One of the tough things about being friends with Conner was that he was so vibrant and always the center of attention. He and I went to school together for years and whenever we would run into one of our former teachers, they would break into a big smile and say "Conner!" and give him a big hug. They would then look at me and just say hi with absolutely no hint of recognition in their eyes.

I would look at them and think, "Really? Really? I was in your class too!"

That was just the way it was. He was just more memorable than everyone else. You couldn't really be angry with him, perhaps a little envious, but never angry and certainly not for long.

-Jonathan Pelzner

He wasn't perfect. He could be annoying and lazy. He could frustrate you for no reason other than the fact that you knew, better than he did, all that he was capable of achieving in life. He exuded bravado but could be crippled by a lack of true self-confidence. He feared failure without understanding how common failure was and how much he could have learned from it. Nonetheless, as time passes, I forget his imperfections and his flaws. I haven't yet forgotten them completely but their import has certainly waned.

What has emerged in their place are the memories of who he really was and my dreams of what he could have been. What remains are recollections of laughter and hugs. What remains are pictures and stories. What remains are echoes and, ultimately, ashes...dry, lifeless ashes.

The arguments and disappointments become, in reflection, abstract and unimportant. What could have been important enough to warrant the heated arguments? Rather than contemplating his failure to achieve the successes we dreamed of for him, we are faced with the questions of whether we could have, and should have, done things differently and if, ultimately, we aren't somehow responsible for his death.

These questions about why Conner didn't achieve greater success are much easier to ask in hindsight. The questions about our culpability become more difficult. Obviously, had we known that Conner would have slightly less than twenty-one years to live his life; we would have done things differently. This wasn't, however, a situation where our child had a terminal disease and a shortened life expectancy. Knowing your child has a limited lifespan gives you a different perspective. In that situation, you are able to focus on the present more than on the distant future. You can treasure the little victories and milestones and recognize them for what they are.

This is not to say that parents of children with terminal illnesses have it any easier than we did, as they most assuredly do not. I can't fathom the pain parents must experience as they watch their child suffer, knowing there is little, if anything, they can do to ease the suffering. They do, however, have a different perspective than do parents who look at their children and anticipate a "normal" lifespan. Most parents accept the trials and tribulations of childhood as part of a process of preparing their children for full adult lives. Most parents can dream of graduations and weddings and grandchildren to come. They can imagine their relationship evolving from that of parent and child to that day when they have an adult relationship with their children. We certainly looked forward to the day when Conner and his sister, Moira, would share the youthful antics and escapades that they had hidden from us during their youths.

When a child's life is cut short, suddenly and unexpectedly, a parent has no choice but to rue the wasted time, opportunities, and lessons that ended up having limited practical use. With extensive reflection, I have come to understand that while I would certainly have done things differently, the fact is that my son had a great, albeit much too short, life. He loved and knew he was loved. He laughed and caused others to laugh. He experienced joy and brought joy to others.

The purpose of this book is not to glorify Conner or to make him anything other than what he was. What he was, and what he will always be, is my son. My memories may be selective at times. My characterization of him may be slanted and more subjective than objective. So be it. If I choose to forget the dark periods in lieu of remembering the good times, and to forget the tears in lieu of the laughter, then that is exactly what I will do—without apology or embarrassment.

Conner Patrick Luby was a lot of things to a lot of people and I certainly hope to paint a big enough picture to address at least some of what he was, not just to myself but to all those whose lives he touched. He possessed certain gifts that I suspect he knew about but may not have fully understood or appreciated. These were gifts that allowed him to touch many lives and to accumulate an incredibly diverse collection of friends and acquaintances. These gifts allowed him to connect with people of varying ages, intellects, and interests.

It's not that he was the smartest person in the room, the most athletic, or even the best looking. He was certainly intelligent although he underperformed academically. He had a substantial degree of natural athleticism and physical grace but lacked the internal drive and discipline necessary to excel at any particular sport. He was good looking, with his (usually) blond hair, his bright blue eyes, and his beautiful white teeth, but not so good looking as to be intimidating or off-putting.

These attributes were not, however, what made him such a fascinating and captivating personality. They were just the calling card that allowed him to get his foot in the door and make an initial connection with another person. He would then use his humor and charm, and often his sense of the outrageous, to build lasting relationships. He exuded a charisma that drew people to him and made him instantly noticeable, even amidst a crowd. His love of others made it easy to forgive him when he did something stupid and he did a lot of stupid things.

He possessed a sense of joy that was both instant and exuberant. It was infectious. He was one of those people who seemed to physically light up a room with his presence.

I remember taking him for hikes in the woods when he was just a small boy. I saw this as an opportunity to expose him to nature; to instill in him a lifelong love of walking; and to give him a chance to gain an appreciation of the quiet beauty of the Northwest. He, on the other hand, saw these hikes as a chance to talk to his Dad...and other random hikers...and the squirrels...and the trees...and anyone and anything else he might see. He just wanted to talk. His personality was too large to be kept silent. There would be no hiding his light under a bushel. His essence just had to burst out. He filled his life with people, laughter, and music. The joy that he felt just needed to be shared with others, and the sharing only served to magnify his own happiness.

At the prayer vigil on the day after he died, people referred to him as having lived loudly—not large, perhaps not always well, certainly not famously, but loudly. It wasn't that he spoke with a particularly loud voice but, rather, that he was so noticeable and that his actions spoke volumes. If Conner was in the room, you knew it. People were drawn to him because of his smile or the spark in his eyes or his laughter or any combination of those attributes. He would speak to complete strangers and always made an effort to introduce new acquaintances to his friends. His charisma was similar to that of many successful politicians. It was an ability to instantly create a personal bond with other people, a bond strong enough to build into a lasting relationship.

An old friend of mine once told me about meeting former President Bill Clinton on a flight back from China. Although my friend only spoke with Clinton for a couple of hours, he was convinced that they had just formed a strong and enduring bond of friendship. He sincerely believed that in those short, few hours, he had become an official "Friend of Bill's." He never spoke with Clinton again, but that did not diminish the fact that the two of them had formed this special bond that he still treasures to this day.

Conner had that same ability. Once you knew Conner, once you connected with him, you felt as if you had that special bond with him, even if you might not see him again for months or even years. The bond was such that you knew, no matter how long of a gap there might be, that Conner would breeze back into your life sometime in the future – most likely when you least expected and often when you most needed. He became infamous for random and frequent late night telephone calls and texts. He never objected to a late night conversation with anyone who needed to talk to a friend. For him, disagreements were merely momentary disruptions of friendships; once a friendship was formed, it was forever. There was no stretch of time too long or distance too far to sunder a friendship, once established.

He projected his charisma primarily through his eyes, which seemed to almost twinkle with both glee and mischievousness and always sought out others, as well as his smile, which conveyed a wide range of emotions. He would display a sheepish grin if caught in some harmless prank or lie or a sly smile if he thought he might put something over on you. Most commonly, however, his face showed pure, unmitigated delight at seeing something or someone who brought him happiness. It was difficult to respond to him with anything other than a smile right back at him and to share in his love of the moment. His joy was as infectious as it was frequent.

I can still see him positively bursting with ecstasy when he successfully pulled off a surprise eighteenth birthday party for his friend Megan McAninch. He planned the party for weeks and went to great lengths to keep it a surprise from her. When she walked in and he took the blindfold off of her eyes, he was even more overjoyed than Megan. The fact that he had been able to bring such happiness to someone so important to him absolutely exhilarated him. His excitement was so great that he erupted in a series of spastic leaps and hollers.

He was not, of course, constantly happy. We took a vacation to Cape Cod when Conner was sixteen years old. He was just at that age when he was too young to be of much interest to his older cousins but too old to want to hang with his parents and little sister. His boredom quickly evolved into surliness as he was out of his element. One afternoon I announced that we were all driving up to Provincetown for the evening. He told me he didn't want to go but I wasn't about to let him sulk at home by himself.

For anyone not familiar with Provincetown, it is a very peculiar place. It has long been a Mecca for the gay community and teems with curious little shops, gay bars, and historical sites. First and foremost, it is a tourist town and tourists drive its economy. I had been to Provincetown countless times in my youth and always felt safe there. I had no concern about exposing my children to the culture of the town.

We drove up and Conner was mostly quiet while the rest of us were chatting away. We had to park a ways from downtown and Conner was almost muttering as we started walking to the downtown area. Within minutes, Cher pulled up on a Razor scooter. Of course, it really wasn't Cher but, rather, a thin and tall drag queen in full Cher regalia. She was very chatty and invited us to a drag show that evening.

I looked at Conner and, for just a moment, he was completely perplexed. I asked "Cher" if we could have our picture taken with her and she agreed. She promptly sidled up to Conner, as he was the best looking of us, and I took a picture.

In that moment, Conner realized how much fun and outrageous Provincetown could be. He had no questions about his sexuality and saw this as just another new experience and opportunity for fun. That evening, we saw countless drag queens of all sizes and colors and, without exception, all of them were friendly and outgoing, especially to the cute sixteen year old boy walking with his family. Strolling down the main street, we saw a store called *Spank The Monkey* and took a picture of Conner in front of it, with him giving the camera a solid two thumbs up gesture.

He was once again the fun and extroverted son that I had grown to know and love. While he would always consider himself to be a West

Coast kind of guy, he now knew that he could enjoy himself anywhere. The world was just starting to open up for him.

This is the Conner whom I choose to remember. This is the Conner that I will always remember; open (albeit sometimes reluctantly) to new experiences; mostly fun and always fun-loving.

While his love of life might have been his most obvious attribute, his innate sense of right and wrong is tougher to describe but probably more important to figuring out who he was. I won't say that he was a saint, for he surely wasn't. He did, however, have a strong and deeply personal moral compass and always spoke up when necessary to help others. Conner was not one to sit by and let another be bullied or abused. He was not one to allow others to drift through life friendless. He was not one to allow someone to get lost in social discomfort and estrangement.

During his freshman year of high school, Conner, of course, immediately bonded with a number of his classmates and instinctively knew where, and with whom, to sit in the cafeteria for lunch. During the first week of school, Conner looked over to the doorway of the cafeteria and saw another freshman boy. This young man was substantially overweight and had mottled skin. He didn't seem to know where to sit. In other words, he didn't know where, or even whether, he would fit into the maelstrom of high school life.

Conner walked up to his new classmate and looked him in the eye, paused a moment, and then said, "Cancer, huh?"

"Yeah," the young man replied, warily.

Conner then replied with a simple, but exuberant, "Cool!" He took the young man by the arm and brought him back to his table. This classmate, Jason, was recovering from leukemia and the steroid treatment had caused his weight gain. The mottled skin was caused by vitiligo, the loss of the melanocytes in the skin from the chemotherapy. Conner immediately gave him a couple of nicknames that he would keep for years. Those nicknames included "Leukie Boy," "Cancer," and "Cancer Fuck." If Conner saw him from a distance, he would yell out, "Hey,

Cancer, c'mon over!"

I got to know Jason pretty well over the years and, for at least the first couple of years, I only knew him as "Leukie Boy." It wasn't until he was a junior in high school that I would start calling him by his true name. Jason seemed to revel in the nicknames because they signified his entry into a group of friends, an opportunity that might not have otherwise been available to him.

What I most enjoy about this story is that Conner reacted to someone who was in an uncomfortable situation—uncomfortable for Jason, as well as for his other classmates—who didn't know what to say or how to act around him. It is not just kids who have difficulty addressing differences and difficult situations; but it is often harder for them because they have less experience with such differences and situations. What a rare gift it was for Conner to not just address that discomfort but to embrace it.

The nicknames he gave to Jason were not intended to mock him but, rather, to mock the diseases he suffered from and the social discomfort they created. Conner saw someone in need and, instead of avoiding the "elephant in the room," he embraced it. Differences did not make him uncomfortable because he found differences to be interesting. He seemed to innately understand that the best way to diffuse an uncomfortable situation is through humor. By mocking Jason's cancer, he allowed Jason and his classmates to build friendships as kids, without awkwardness. The nicknames were a way of putting everyone at ease and making it understood that Jason was just like everyone else, albeit with a different set of problems, and, as such, could be teased just like everyone else.

I want to add that Jason experienced a complete recovery from the leukemia and, after graduation from high school, became a personal trainer and a CrossFit competitor. He has turned into a remarkable person in his own right. Jason was a regular in our home throughout his high school years and was very important to all of us in the period just after Conner's death. Unfortunately, without Conner to act as the glue that maintained our relationship, we have drifted apart and have not spoken in years. He will, however, always have a special place in our hearts.

* * *

Conner was always faithful to his own personal moral code. A girl he worked with was dating one of Conner's good friends and apparently the boyfriend got physically abusive. While Conner's friendship had been stronger with the boyfriend, he immediately took the girlfriend's side and defended her. He kicked the boyfriend out of the hookah bar where Conner worked and cussed him out for hitting a girl.

One of our hard and fast family rules was, *you never hit girls...EVER!* After chewing out the boyfriend, Conner took the time to provide a sympathetic shoulder to the girl. He never hesitated a moment to consider what effect this might have on his friendship with the boyfriend. Right was right and wrong was wrong. Hitting a girl was wrong. Nothing else really mattered.

This girl told me that, after the incident of abuse, all of her old friends abandoned her and took the side of the boyfriend. Conner was the only one to stand by her. He was willing to sacrifice a friendship in order to assert what he knew was right. It was that important. He could not, and would not, leave this young woman alone. While there was never any romantic relationship between them, he knew what he had to do and he did it.

This young woman explained to me how important Conner's support was to her. It allowed her to maintain and build upon her own sense of self-worth. It showed her how to be a friend to others and to make the right decision even when it is not the easiest decision.

Over time, Conner and the boyfriend became friends once again. A year or so after Conner's death, the boyfriend approached me and told me how he had given up drinking and was working on doing something with his life. He attributed much of this change to Conner and the fact that Conner was willing to make that stand. He now understood what he had done wrong and wanted to be more like Conner.

A couple of years ago, another young woman called my office to make an appointment for a legal consultation. She told me on the phone that she wanted to discuss an employment issue. When the day came, she walked into my office and I realized immediately that she was, or at some point had been, a man.

We discussed her issue for a while and I gave her the appropriate legal advice. As she was leaving, I finally spoke up. "I just have to ask, how did you get my name?"

"Your son." She smiled at me. "I went to school with Conner."

She was obviously waiting to see if I recognized her or might at least have heard of her. My face was a blank because, in fact, I didn't recognize her and I couldn't remember any stories of a transvestite or transgender person at Jesuit High School. Seeing the look on my face, she continued, "Life at Jesuit was not always easy for me but your son was always very kind. I just wanted to let you know that you raised a good boy."

I shook her hand and, as she left, I wiped my eyes but it was futile.

It is immensely satisfying to me to hear these stories about my son and to know that he took to heart so many of the life lessons we taught him. These lessons weren't wasted as a result of the premature end of his life. He applied these lessons every day and made life better for himself and others. What more could a parent ask for, other than for more time with him and more time *for* him?

As I said, I am proud of the boy he was and the man he was becoming. I'm not proud of some of the mistakes that he made, and certainly not the mistake he made in the early morning hours of September 12, 2009. I am, however, proud that I had the opportunity to be his Dad and spend a lifetime—even if only his lifetime—with him.

chapter three
the family

I believe Conner's traits came from the close family ties he kept over the years. Like himself, his family has a heart of gold. A valuable lesson that Conner taught me was that no matter what you were going through, always fight for family first. I stand by that rule to this day and I still lean on him in times of need. Though Conner is stubborn as a mule when it comes to rules, he could never bear to let down his family. This is one of the many traits that makes Conner who he is... or was.

-Fallon Hawk

I had a great childhood, truly a wonderful childhood, filled with little regret or lasting disappointment. Being the youngest of six children left me free, for the most part, of responsibility, supervision, and parental expectations. We were a middle-class family, or perhaps more accurately, an upper-middle-class family. My parents were good people and just good enough parents to let me grow but, more importantly, to allow me to recognize the areas that I, as a parent someday, would want to improve upon. I will always be grateful to my father for imparting a love of words and wordplay to me, as well as a sense of humor that could range from lowbrow and crass to clever and sophisticated. I will always be grateful to my mother for teaching me that love requires the ability to look beyond a person's flaws and imperfections.

My father, while possessing numerous flaws and imperfections that my mother had to look beyond, always seemed larger than life. He was intelligent and loud and never one to shy away from stating his opinions or telling a joke. One of my favorites stories, and one that epitomized him, involved an incident he had with a local judge. My father was an attorney and, one day, appeared in front of this judge when the judge was in a bad mood. Now I never really found out if it was truly the judge's bad mood or if my father was just unprepared for the hearing; but, apparently, the judge made a particular effort to embarrass my father in front of his client. Understanding the decorum necessary in court, my father accepted the abuse with discipline and restraint.

Just a week or so later, the Boston College Law School Board of Trustees met. My father had been on the Board for a number of years and knew all the other Trustees. The newest Trustee happened to be the same judge who had embarrassed him just a short time before, and the judge only knew one other person on the Board—my father.

Accordingly, the judge sidled up to my father as he was talking to a few people. My father graciously introduced the judge to the people he was talking to and then walked away and started talking to a couple of the other trustees.

The judge followed my father and, again, my father graciously introduced the judge to these Trustees and then walked away. This happened a time or two more before the judge understood that my father wasn't going to spend any time talking to him or provide him with a familiar face to dine with.

The following Monday, my father was in the courthouse and happened to run into the judge's clerk. The clerk said, "You better watch out, Luby, the judge is really pissed at you."

My father calmly looked at the clerk and said, "You go back to the judge and tell him that I am every bit as fucking Irish as he is!" He and the judge never had a problem with one another after that.

* * *

Growing up, I was reasonably intelligent, moderately good-looking but generally timid and lacking any semblance of athleticism or self-confidence. My siblings shared many of these same basic traits but there was a substantial variance in looks, intelligence, and sociability among the six of us. One characteristic that seemed to run in the family, although to a different degree with each of us, was a deficiency of common sense. Many of us failed to learn from our mistakes or the mistakes of other family members. Some of us failed to grasp the difference between what most families were really like as opposed to the idealized families of our imaginations and the network television of the early 1960s. Our family was dysfunctional but, in comparison to other families I have observed, not unduly so. We were close in age, with six kids spread out over eight years, but with the exception of the two eldest sisters, we were not unusually close in friendship. Nonetheless, the oldest two sisters seemed to take a particular interest in helping to raise my brother and me, Christine providing additional mothering to Jed and Maureen to me. They counseled and protected us, as best they could, and in many ways were more involved in our early years than our parents were.

Coming from a large family of strong personalities and being the youngest, I spent much of my childhood as the "son of..." or "little brother of..." This was particularly rankling to me with regards to my brother. Jed was two years older than me and was everything I wanted to be as a teenager but wasn't. He was handsome, resembling a young Jim Morrison, athletic, musical, and both confident and successful with girls. His strengths just seemed to amplify my deficiencies. And I loved him and envied him.

At the time, I didn't realize how growing up in his shadow, as well as that of my Dad, was limiting my growth and my future. I couldn't compete with either of them and could never develop my own identity living with them. The amazing thing to me, in retrospect, is that I didn't realize at the time how much I was living in their shadows. It was comfortable because it was known. Even if I was only Jim Luby's son or Jed Luby's little brother, I was still someone. I had no concept of crawling out of their shadows and no understanding of what I might be capable of on my own. The thought of living away from family and friends, the thought of going outside of my comfort zone, was not something I ever even considered.

When it came time to head off to college, I only looked at schools in New England. With my limited ambition, I headed off to Providence College for my first year of college. I chose Providence College for two simple reasons: first of all, it was relatively close to home; secondly, they accepted me. I found that even going just sixty miles away to Providence, Rhode Island was a difficult transition.

As with any other change, it took a while for me to adapt to a larger school, new friends, and greater independence. It was difficult to develop any sort of comfort level when surrounded by so many people from different towns and even states. None of these people knew my Dad. None of these people knew my brother or any of my other siblings. I had to start defining myself.

Early in my freshman year and shortly after my eighteenth birthday, I had a revelation. I realized that up to that point in my life, I had never been farther west than New York City nor farther south than Washington, D.C., and I had only been to those cities once each. In this revelation, I came to understand that this was somehow wrong. With a maturity and prescience that surprised me and was previously unknown, I understood that if I didn't get away from New England while in college, I likely never would. I finally understood that I had to crawl out from the shade of the family tree if there was ever to be a chance for me to find out what I was really capable of. Certainly I might return to New England someday but, if I did, I wanted it to be because it was my choice rather than just because it was all I knew. For the first time in my life, I refused to allow my fear of the unknown to limit my options. I refused to allow my dependence upon my family to continue. It was time to find out what was outside of my comfortable little world.

Fortunately, two good friends of mine were attending Regis College in Denver. Without really consulting my parents or siblings but, rather, just notifying them of my decision, I transferred there beginning my sophomore year. If they cared that I was moving so far away, they never said anything. In any event, that single decision opened up the world to me. From there, I was able to spend a semester in Spain and then, after graduation, move to Houston. In Houston, I first worked at a desk job for an insurance company but quickly realized that I was not yet ready for that type of tedium. After only one year, I quit and began waiting tables and tending bar. I worked a lot and I worked hard but, most importantly at that point in my life, I had fun. I had finally developed the confidence to be able to make decisions and accept their consequences. Finally, I was developing into who I was and who I was meant to be.

After a couple of years of tending bar and dating every available waitress I could, and feeling my brain start to atrophy, I decided to go to law school. I had resisted the notion of becoming a lawyer for most of my life. My father was a lawyer and *his* father had been a well-respected, and even feared, judge. I always knew that law school was an option but not one that I was particularly drawn to. Knowing, however, that I needed to do something with my life and not knowing what else to do, I decided to give it a shot.

I ended up at Notre Dame School of Law, again for two reasons. The first was that I knew it was more of a national, rather than regional, law school so I would have greater flexibility as to where I ended up when I settled down. Secondly, and perhaps most importantly, they accepted me.

I would be heading to Northern Indiana, a place that I had never been to and one I knew almost nothing about. I had not grown up following college football and I knew little about Notre Dame other than it was well-respected, with a strong reputation for academic excellence. The fact that it was a Catholic institution had no relevance one way or the other. Unlike when I transferred from Providence College to Regis College, I had no trepidation about moving to unknown Indiana. I had discovered that moving to a new region of the country was the type of adventure that now appealed to me.

I still remember my first weekend at Notre Dame, going through orientation. At one point, I took a walk through the campus with one of the prettier girls in our class, Karen Covey. During this stroll, she said to me, "I'll just die if I ever get a B."

I looked at her with bewilderment. "Karen, you'll drive yourself crazy with that kind of thinking," I told her. " You need to remember that all of us are used to all, or at least mostly, A's. That is how we got here. Personally, I don't care if I graduate with a 4.0 or a 3.0; all I care about is that I graduate."

Shortly before writing this book, I reconnected with Karen and reminded her of that story. She confirmed for me that she had, in fact, gotten a B or two, yet had not only survived but also flourished. Similarly, I got a B or two (or more), and maybe even a C or two (or more), but also survived and flourished.

It was during my second year of law school that the need for both money and an escape from the occasional dreariness of academia inspired me to look for a part-time job. I landed a position as a bartender at a newly-opened restaurant called "Senor Kelly's." It was an unnatural and unwieldy combination of an Irish bar and Mexican restaurant. As far as I was concerned, it was only notable for the fact that it employed a really cute cocktail waitress who I began to fancy. Jane Kessel was dating someone else at the time but I quickly swept her off of her feet and thirty-plus years later, we are still together.

* * *

The decision to move to Portland, Oregon after graduation was also an interesting process. At that point in my life, I did not want to return to New England. I had grown to like the fact that I was my own person rather than being known solely as my parents' son or my siblings' little brother. While I certainly loved my parents and my siblings, my preference was to love them from a distance, a substantial distance. I suspect that they may have shared this preference and certainly never disagreed with my decision.

Jane didn't want to stay in the Midwest as she shared my belief in loving one's family best from a distance. Neither of us was overly fond of the idea of living in the South as we had no affinity for heat or humidity. In the summer between my second and third years of law school, we took a trip out West. During the Los Angeles portion of the trip, we went to a beach at Will Rogers State Park. While there, I saw a girl in a tiny bikini who was absolutely stunning. The fact that she couldn't have been more than thirteen years old made it kind of creepy. Right then and there, I realized that California wasn't for me. I didn't want that to be my daughter in another fifteen years or so. We just weren't Southern California-type people. We were the type of people that Southern California-type people make fun of for being boring and living a lifestyle involving white picket fences and lazy summer afternoons. We were the type of people to have well-behaved children who favored modesty over flash and substance over form. It is more than a bit ironic that Conner eventually developed the persona of a surfer dude with bleached blonde hair and a laconic manner more common to the beaches of Southern California than the flannel-clad environs of the Northwest.

On that same trip out West, we also visited Portland and Seattle and loved both cities. The size and climate of the Northwest was just right for us. Of course we visited in the summertime and didn't realize how gray and rainy winters could be. While I had a slight preference for Seattle, I deferred to Jane and she chose Portland. She liked the fact that Portland was the smaller of the two cities and seemed to have a more relaxed feel to it. With thirty years of hindsight, it turned out to be the right decision.

Jane and I married on September 15, 1984, and things moved pretty quickly. I got my first attorney job as soon as I passed the Bar exam. Niehaus, Hanna, Murphy, Green, Osaka & Dunn, a small firm that was rapidly outgrowing its name partners, hired me. My starting annual salary of $24,000 was enough to allow Jane to go back to school and get her associate's degree as an orthodontic assistant. We settled into a life of domesticity and suddenly developed thoughts of purchasing our first house.

Like other young married couples, we often went out on weekends and looked at houses. We had no money saved and Jane was still in school, so it was more wishful thinking than real house hunting. Then, one day, we stumbled upon an older, bungalow-style home that was vacant and for sale. The home had a "blind assumable" mortgage, which meant that we didn't have to qualify for the loan. Rather, the seller could just assign the loan over to us and the house would be ours.

We bought the house for $56,000 and moved in. It was definitely a fixer-upper and that is what Jane and I did. We ripped out walls, re-wired, re-plumbed, painted, and did most of the work ourselves. We recruited friends to help replace dry-rotted wood and rusted pipes. We hosted painting parties to help fix up the house. My dad came for a visit and taught me how to replace the sash cords in the windows.

Once we were settled in the house and had made it into our home, we decided that it was time to start having kids. Almost from the time we first fell in love with one another, Jane and I knew that we wanted to have children. We sensed in each other the instincts and abilities that would allow us to be good parents. We sensed that our differing strengths would balance out our respective shortcomings. While be both loved our parents, we knew that we could be better parents than they had been. After all, isn't that the trick to parenting? Figure out what your parents did well and copy them. Figure out what they didn't do well and do things differently. After being together for almost four years, it was time.

Unfortunately, the decision to conceive was much easier than the actual conception. We tried and tried, to no avail. We started going to a fertility specialist and Jane began taking fertility drugs. We maintained an ovulation chart and started to schedule our lovemaking. There is nothing that kills the romance of conceiving a child quite like having to schedule intercourse.

Finally, in December 1987, Jane surprised me by telling me that she was pregnant. Less than a week later, however, she miscarried. I wish I could convey our disappointment and frustration. Suffice it to say, it was not our last, joint experience with despair.

Our fertility doctor told us that we should wait before starting again in order to let Jane's body return to normal. Being young and married to an incredibly beautiful woman, patience proved better in theory than in practice. In February 1988, Jane went back to the doctor and found out that she was, again, pregnant. We were going to be parents.

chapter four
the mourning comes

I was really hungover, like super, super hungover. I had just started this new job and I was teaching dance to three- and four-year-olds. I tried working that day but was too sick so I went home. Finally I got up to bed and felt absolutely terrible. I'm laying there and just falling asleep when the phone rings. I looked at the phone and saw it was from Caitlyn Lang.

I answered it just because it was so weird that she would be calling me. She was crying and I asked if she was all right. She said, "I just needed to call you because Conner died."

I was trying to process this through the fog in my head and said, "Wait, what are you saying? What are you talking about?"

And she said, "Conner. Conner Luby. He died."

I hung up the phone and just lay there. I didn't know what to do. I didn't even know what to feel.

-Hannah Frazier
née Russell

I stood there with the phone to my ear, trying to make sense of the words. As soon as they did, my mind became instantly hyperalert even as it spun in a million different directions at once. I had to make an instantaneous decision as to what to do next. Jane knew from the sound of my voice and the look on my face that something was wrong, seriously wrong.

I told Moira to "put him on," referring to the policeman. It was, in fact, the Deputy Medical Examiner and he gave me a quick rundown of what had happened. He told me that Conner had died that morning after driving into the back of a construction truck. I'm sure he told me more but, at that instant in time, I was looking at Jane and watching her face fill with alarm. Whatever further he might have said just didn't register. At that point, all I knew was that our son was dead. Jane was starting to suspect the worst without truly understanding how bad the worst could be. I could see the panic starting to overwhelm her.

You hear people talk about how, during times of high stress, time seems to slow, and even stop. It does. You hear people talk about how, during times of high stress, your mind seems to focus to a degree otherwise unknown. It does.

Unfortunately, the stress also requires you to compartmentalize portions of your psyche. You have to shut down your emotions and distance yourself from the immediacy and intensity of the pain. You have to focus solely on the here and now rather than the past or the future. This is exactly what I did.

As I hung up the phone, using a flat monotone to tell the Deputy Medical Examiner that we would be right home, I looked at Jane. I wish I could remember exactly what I said to her—how I broke the news to her that her only son was dead. I know that I was awkward and stiff, having already slipped into a degree of emotional detachment I had never experienced before. I know that I was incapable of providing the tact and comfort that I otherwise would have, and should have, provided. A flat monotone was all I could muster. I told her something about Conner being in a car accident and dying. She collapsed on the bed, repeating, "No! No! No!"

I could not comfort her. My mind was swirling with decisions to be made and a million different thoughts. I didn't have time to comfort or grieve; neither one of us did. This was neither the time nor the place for that. We had to get home. We had to get to Moira.

As the realization quickly set in, Jane's sobs slowed to a stop and she just stared at me. Her eyes were beseeching me to tell her that this was a mistake, that Conner was all right. I could only stare back and say, "I'm sorry. I'm so, so sorry."

Like a door suddenly slamming shut, we both stood up, shuttered our emotions, and got on with what needed to be done. We quickly started throwing things in our suitcases, and I ran downstairs to check out of the Stephanie Inn.

There was a small line at the front desk clerk as people checked in or out. I stood patiently for about twenty seconds, and then the urgency became too much. I moved to the front of the line and said, "Excuse me, we have to check out right away. We've had an emergency at home." The clerk looked at me and, without hesitation, asked for my room number. He did not make any other inquiries and I am still not sure if he was acting from standard protocol or if he reacted to something he saw in my face. In any event, he immediately checked me out.

While I felt as if I was somewhat in control, the panic frayed the edges of my composure, much as you might imagine a single thread slowly unraveling an entire sweater. Each minute, each second was one more tug on that thread.

As I was walking back to the stairs, one of the other guests came up to me and asked if I was okay. I told him that we had just gotten a call that our son died in a car accident. The look on his face must have mirrored mine, for he physically staggered back a step as if hit by a brick. I vaguely heard him say, "I'm so sorry," but I had already turned away and was heading back up the stairs to our room.

As I ran into the room, Jane and I snuck plaintive looks at one another but said nothing. We both recognized how fragile our emotions were and didn't want to say anything that would cause the other to crack, at least not then, not yet. I grabbed whatever bags I could and ran them down to the car. Jane stayed in the room, gathering the last of our belongings and throwing them into our remaining suitcase. After that first trip to the car, I called Tony DiCioccio. I felt an overwhelming need to tell someone, someone who knew me and who knew Conner.

I needed to share my grief, albeit just a little bit. I knew I couldn't open the door to grief very far or I wouldn't be able to do what needed to be done. Tony was Conner's godfather; had been the best man in our wedding; and had been one of my best friends for longer than I care to remember.

When he answered the phone, I could barely manage to squeak out, "Tony, Conner was killed in a car accident last night. I'll call you later." I then hung up before he could respond.

When I say that my voice squeaked, it really did. I remember my vocal cords tightening up and having to fight to get the words out. This required me to again force the grief away, to keep my emotions from overwhelming me. This had become more than just an emotional struggle; it was now affecting me physically as well.

As we hurriedly finished packing and throwing things into the car, Jane and I engaged in a short debate as to who would drive home. Jane is a more aggressive driver than I am but I am generally a safer driver. Knowing how fragile we both were, I decided that I needed to drive. We couldn't risk getting into an accident. We couldn't risk any potential delay in getting home. Even more importantly, we couldn't risk costing Moira her parents to a car accident on the same day that she lost her brother. Jane didn't put up much of a fight. I think she was just too overwhelmed at that point to argue.

On the drive home, while I was driving as quickly as I could, we started making phone calls. We called my brother in New Hampshire because my mother and sisters, Maureen and Nancy, were there for a vacation. I couldn't handle talking to everyone, so I left it to him to break the news to the rest of the family.

Jane called her sister in Canton, Ohio, and her best friend, Roni Sidman. We called our friends Kerry and Angie Sisk. I'm sure we called others as well but I'll be damned if I can remember who. Calling others became a way to avoid having to talk to one another. Talking to one another meant opening the wound wide and letting all of the pain in. We weren't ready for that yet. Telling the news to others allowed us to distance ourselves a bit from the horror, if only because we were acting as messengers. With each other, there would be no distance. With each other, there would only be the brutal honesty of what had just happened to our family and the boy we loved so much.

The drive back home took forever and yet passed in an instant. In looking back, my memories of the drive are vague and unsubstantial. Like so many other things that happened over the following week or so, this was like being in a fog where some things were clearly in view while others were just faint outlines and smudges. I know that we called Moira back a couple of times to check on her. She told us that some of the neighbors were there so she wasn't alone. We told her that we loved her and then told her that again and again and again.

At one point during the drive, Jane displayed an emotional strength that I never expected and that still amazes me. In the middle of all the stress and fear, with our emotional stability strained to its limit, she looked at me and said, "We can't let this come between us. We can't be one of those couples who can't survive the loss of a child. We need to stay strong. We need to make sure that you and I make it...together."

I understood exactly what she was talking about but had not even considered that possibility. Over the following years, Jane and I had many opportunities to walk away from each other but neither of us ever did. Conner's death seemed to intensify the normal ebb and flow of marriage. We fought harder than we had previously and the pain, both inflicted and sustained, was more substantial and deeper. Nonetheless, we both knew that we were stronger as a couple than we would be individually. We knew that we were better people together than separately.

We knew that we needed one another.

I remember, while driving 85–90 mph down the highway, thinking about what would happen if a policeman pulled us over. I knew the exact words I was going to say, and I knew that my eyes and my voice would convince the policeman that I was serious and that my speeding was justifiable. In my mind, I saw the policeman leading us home with his lights flashing and siren blaring. In the whole drive from Cannon

Beach to Tigard, almost 100 miles, we didn't see a single police car.

It was a beautiful September morning as we neared our home. The sky was a bright, cloudless blue and the trees were still full and green. People were out mowing their lawns and talking with one another. The soccer fields we drove by were full of children and their parents yelling and laughing. Everything was so full of life. Everything was so normal and ordinary yet everything was so different.

When we finally arrived home, we rushed into the house to see Moira. There were about eight or nine people there. Our neighbor Michelle Addy was there with her daughters. Moira had asked the State Troopers to contact the Addys and have them come over and stay with her while she waited for us. Moira's old friend Cassie and her mom, Leslie Westfall, were also there. Roni Sidman was there. Then I saw Conner's friends Jonathon Pelzner and Jeff Polits sitting there. They were both beyond the ability to cry. Jon looked at us, his eyes seeming to beg us to tell him that this was all just a big mistake. Jeff couldn't even bring himself to look at us, as if doing so would just confirm the worst. While I wanted to comfort both of them, our focus was on Moira.

As tough as it is to lose a child, both Jane and I were old enough to know, at least a little bit, what to expect. We had both lost parents and had had friends die unexpectedly. Many years before, I lost an older sister to cancer. Moira and the boys, however, had never experienced anything like this before. They didn't know what to do; they didn't know what to say; they didn't even know how to feel. They just sat there in a state that might best be described as semicomatose. Jeff, in particular, just stared at the floor, totally lost in his thoughts. It was only in the coming months and years that we learned how deeply Jeff had been affected by Conner's death. It was through Jeff, more than anyone else other than Moira, that we learned what Conner meant to people.

Moira's behavior was both reassuring and disturbing. She was preternaturally calm. While she was clearly in shock, she remained coherent and had a sense of strength that we hadn't noticed before. She seemed to understand, much as I did, that this was not the time or the place to grieve. For all of us - Jane, Moira, and myself—grief was to be primarily a private experience. We maintained a strong public face. We knew that others would look to us for their cue as to how to act, how to respond, and how to grieve. Moira, at sixteen years of age, already seemed to inherently sense and understand that our role in this unfolding drama was to provide emotional support and comfort to others. We would subvert and delay our grief. We would don the mask of emotional strength, a mask that was uncomfortable and unwieldy but necessary.

chapter five

jean pierre

We met through our love and passion for music. Conner introduced himself online after stumbling upon my band's music. After months of touring, we finally made our way up to the beautiful Northwest. Conner was the first person to reach out and try to help five smelly band boys from Arizona feel a little closer to home with his hospitality. He offered us the food and comfort of his own parents' home even though I'm still not sure if his parents ever knew of his kind gesture.

Needless to say, he was quite the friend. The kind of friend that would show up hours early to help us load-in our heavy gear, show us the good places to eat by the venue, then take us around the town at night.

The day I heard of his passing was the same day we were playing a festival show in Flagstaff, Az. We learned of the accident a few minutes before we went on and were crushed. With heavy hearts, we got ourselves together and dedicated the entire set to the great man, and my great friend, Conner Luby. I will forever miss him.

-Johnny Abdullah,
Bassist, A Change of Pace

As many parents know and understand, pregnancy—especially after a miscarriage—is a fearful experience, at least until you hear a heartbeat. Accordingly, we hid the news and our growing excitement from both friends and family. Eventually, of course, we did hear the heartbeat and it was such a magical experience to hear that "whooshing" sound and know that it was our child's heart beating; to know that our future was bound up in that tiny little heart. It was a life that we were responsible for creating; a life that we would forever nurture and protect. If I had to pick the first moment when I considered myself a father, it was then.

Like most expecting parents, that first real pregnancy was a wonder. We took monthly photos of Jane's ever-expanding belly. I learned to massage her feet after they began to swell from gestational diabetes. We relished the ultrasounds so we could again hear the heartbeat and see the grainy images of a developing human being—*our* human being. We reveled in the hiccups and movements we could feel.

We also, of course, struggled with names. We were looking for something different but not too unusual. We liked the idea of celebrating my Irish heritage. We would have also celebrated Jane's Polish and German heritage but just couldn't see having a child named Kasmir or Olaf or Helmut. We went through a number of Irish names before finally settling on Conner if "he" turned out to be a boy. Of course, we hadn't agreed upon the spelling. Jane liked "Conn*or*" and I preferred "Conn*er*." We thought about using Jane's maiden name as his middle name but decided that "Conner Kessel Luby" sounded too much like a law firm. We settled on Conner Patrick Luby, even though we hadn't really settled on the spelling of the first name.

During the time that we were discussing and debating baby names, we realized that we had to start calling him something. What do you call the person developing within? Referring to him as "the baby," "it," or "the fetus" was all too impersonal and certainly not the way we did things. We decided to give him a pre-natal name, a moniker to use while he was still safely tucked away in Jane's uterus. We decided to call him "Jean Pierre."

I'm still not sure where we came up with that name since neither of us has any French blood in us, but the name stuck. A friend suggested that it was because "chicks dig French guys," but I'm not sure that that was it. It certainly *might* have been, but the more likely reason is just that it was odd and so atypical for the families we came from. Accordingly, it was perfect for us.

Thereafter I would wake Jane in the morning by asking how she and Jean Pierre were doing that day. When he got restless and started kicking, we would talk to Jean Pierre and try and settle him down. When reporting developments to friends and family, we always referred to him as Jean Pierre.

Over the following months, Jean Pierre grew and we did all of the stereotypical things. We fixed up his room and bought all of the necessary baby furniture and supplies. We also babyproofed the house by installing safety plugs in the outlets and latches on drawers well before he was even born. Apparently, we thought that he would be crawling and getting into things as soon as he was born. We were wrong, of course, but not by much.

Jane's labor started on Monday, October 24, 1988, which was a beautiful fall morning. I had just showered and come back into our bedroom to get my clothes and then head off to work. As soon as I walked into the room, Jane said, "I think I'm in labor."

It is difficult to remember or fully explain the combination of excitement and fear that this statement can generate for first-time parents. All the fear and excitement of the preceding eight-plus months coalesce in a froth of nervousness and bravado. The next day and a half were to be both, and simultaneously, boring and overwhelming. The dilation progressed very slowly; physically, Jane did not handle labor well. Her blood pressure rose and she was severely nauseated by the medications used to control her blood pressure. The doctors punctured her amniotic sac and gave her Pitocin to speed up the labor. They gave her Prostaglandin to soften her cervix. She had IVs, a blood pressure cuff, and a fetal monitor. She was miserable and progress was painfully slow.

On the early evening of the 25th, it was time for a serious talk with our obstetrician. At that point, Jane had been in labor for over a day and a half and was obviously still hours away from being fully dilated. He recommended that we proceed with a Caesarian section since the coming of Jean Pierre was proceeding so slowly. We were exhausted, so we quickly agreed. Jane was prepped for surgery and off we went.

Shortly after 7:00 p.m., and after a full thirty-seven hours of labor, Jean Pierre popped his bloody little head out of Jane's belly. I should mention that we still hadn't agreed as to the spelling of Conner's first name. After he was born, the nurse asked us what his name was and how to spell it. Jane was nearly unconscious from all of the stress and anesthesia so I answered "Conner. C-O-N-N-E-R." That would not be the last time she regretted leaving a decision to me.

* * *

One of the first things I did after Conner was born was to hold him—just hold him. I would count, and re-count, and count again, his ten little toes and ten little fingers. I would stare at his little pug nose and head misshapen by childbirth. Now I'm a pretty sentimental guy and I kept waiting for some overwhelming rush of pure love to engulf me, but it didn't. I was expecting something akin to that feeling of infatuation I had experienced when I first started to date Jane. I heard about this rush and read about it but, much to my disappointment, I just didn't feel it. Maybe it was because I was just so tired and drained of emotion by that point in time. Maybe I was overwhelmed by the realization that I was responsible for this new human being. Who he was and who he would become had become my primary responsibility, and I understood, or at least thought I understood, the extent and enormity of that responsibility. Of course, I loved him but there was no warm, fuzzy feeling to experience and wonder at. It was more of a rational, semi-well-thought-out recognition of a new fact. I knew that I was bound to him and hoped that my love for him would grow as he did, but I was disappointed that I didn't experience that much romanticized feeling of love at first sight.

I'm not sure when, exactly, the overwhelming feeling of love finally kicked in. I suspect that it was a gradual bonding that happened over the years and grew increasingly stronger, but there was no one moment when the light bulb turned on. Rather, it was a slow and gradual process that accumulated like the memories. I'm not sure I ever really under-stood the depth and breadth of my love for him, at least not until the call from Moira on that sunny September morning. I knew that I loved him, but just didn't realize how much.

In any event, after helping to give him his first bath, we retreated to our room where Jane was sleeping and recuperating from the grueling labor. It was then, with him cradled in my lap, that I wrote a letter to him. The letter was to be part of a time capsule that we were preparing for him. The capsule would be opened on his eighteenth birthday and would contain artifacts from his birth—an *Oregonian* newspaper from the day of his birth and then-current issues of *Time* and *Playboy*. As it was a presidential election year, we put in artifacts from the 1988 Bush-Du-kakis presidential campaigns. The key thing for me, however, was the letter. I was addressing the letter to an eighteen year-old boy that I didn't yet know.

I didn't know who or what he would be. I didn't know what Con-ner, at age eighteen, would think of us. I even knew that it was possible that I might not be around on his eighteenth birthday. I wanted to help him understand, however, who we were when he was born. I thought it important for him to understand that the parents he would know as an eighteen-year-old man were different from the young and nervous parents of a newborn. I wanted him to know the people in our lives, and hence in his life, at the time he was born. I knew that friendships wax and wane and that people would come and go in our lives. So I wrote the letter and sealed it in his time capsule where we wouldn't read it again for eighteen years; not until his 18th birthday. This is the letter:

10-25-88

Dear Conner Patrick:

As I'm writing this, I'm holding you in my left arm and staring at you in total awe. So far, you are the perfect baby...you haven't cried very much although you do squirm around a lot. Your mother is still in the recovery room. The purpose of this letter is to let you know how things are (or were) at the time of your birth.

I joined your mother in the operating room as she was getting scrubbed and sedated. I really felt sorry for her as she was so exhausted. You were great when you were born. You cried almost immediately but soon quieted down. In the 4 hours you have been with us so far, you've only cried 4 times; twice when you were stuck with a needle so your blood sugar level could be tested.

As for your appearance, you weighed 7 lbs., 14 ½ oz. and stood 22 ¾ inches. Because of the length of the labor, you had a conehead. Your only other distinguishing features were a round face, furrowed brow and big feet. It's now 11:15 p.m. and your mother is on the phone with your Grandmother Kessel. I'm going to go home and get some sleep and I'll finish this tomorrow.

Well, it's time to start up (and finish) this letter. It's now Friday, the 28th. I've been too busy to finish this before now. On Wednesday night, I stayed with you and your mother until 8:30 pm. When I left, I went to the Memorial Coliseum to watch part of the Def Leppard concert. Uncle Tony left me a backstage pass and I got there about 10 minutes before the show started. I ended up staying through the first encore and I was really impressed. They put on a very good show although my ears are still ringing. That is definitely the last show I go to without earplugs.

Now is where I tell you about the various people in your life. This list should help you get to know who you are and why you are like you are.

Jane Kessel Luby: Your mother is a very pretty and feisty woman. I first met her at Señor Kelly's in South Bend. It was just opening in September, 1982 and your Mom was a cocktail waitress and I was a bartender. We quickly became friends and she came over and cut my hair. She invited me to a wedding. We really had a nice time and I then invited her to the ND/ Air Force football game. In late October, we went up to Chicago to visit your Uncle David and Aunt Laura. Lindsay was born less than a month later. It was about then that we officially became an "item."

Your mother is really wonderful. She is the first woman I've ever known with whom I feel completely comfortable. Her sense of humor is as warped as mine. She's very feisty and it'll be interesting to see if your birth will give her more patience.

Kevin Walter Luby: If I had to describe myself right now, I would say that I am a frustrated jock who enjoys being tough at work and fun at home. I'm not a particularly exciting guy but I have my moments. I just hope that I can be the best dad possible for you.

Grandma Kessel: Your maternal grandmother is a piece of work. She is one of the most self-centered people I've ever met. I never knew your grandfather but your mother was his favorite and Laura was your grandmother's favorite. Your mother always ends up agitated and aggravated whenever she's around her mother.

Step-Grandpa Bartley: John is a nice guy although I don't know him that well. He appears willing to put up with your grandmother's crap and be happy about it.

Grandpa Luby: My guess is that you'll never know your paternal grandfather just as I never knew mine. He's a good man although he certainly has his faults. He was a good, but not great, lawyer who made a mistake in borrowing funds from an estate that he was probating. He was caught and convicted and shortly thereafter left Framingham for good. He was so ashamed that he had besmirched the Luby name.

As I write this, your grandfather has cancer. About a year ago, he had cancer of the bladder removed, together with a tumor in his colon and skin cancer on his nose. About two weeks ago, he was diagnosed as having more cancer in the bladder. He has declined an ileostomy and instead opted for experimental chemo and radiation therapy. Because the cancer is of a very aggressive nature, I would be surprised if he lived more than another year or two.

I was never my father's favorite. My brother Jed was as he was tougher, more athletic and more of a ladies' man than I was. He and I, however, have settled into a comfortable relationship that mixes mutual admiration and love.

Grandma Luby: Your paternal grandmother is a nice woman who tends to be a bit bossy. She's been through a lot with my father and deserves the best. I would be surprised if she doesn't last long enough for you to get to know her well.

Aunt Laura: Your mother's sister is hilarious although she can be the pushiest and most self-centered of people. The funny thing however, is the thing that makes her fun, is that she knows that she's pushy and self-centered, and freely admits it.

Uncle David: David is as preppy as they come but has a great personality and is very funny. The way he and Laura like to dance and socialize make me think that they were born 25 years too late. They have the same mindset, as far as cocktails and status, as my parents and their friends. They are good people.

Aunt Chris: My oldest sister drinks too much and eats too much but is as sweet as the day is long. She should have had kids because she would have been a great mother. Although she has the least money of any of the siblings, she is the most generous. She is easily my second favorite sister, right behind your...

Aunt Mo: Maureen helped raise me and we were close all through my childhood. Her first marriage was unfortunate. Michael was generally a nice guy but he was jealous of her and treated her like shit. He was jealous because she came from a better family and was better educated. Like Chris, she would have been a good mother.

Aunt Nancy: Like your Aunt Laura, Nancy is self-centered and pushy, but worse because she won't admit it. Nancy has never made any effort for your mother or anyone else that I know unless she received some direct benefit in return. As you can tell, Nancy is not our favorite. Carlos isn't any better although their kids are great.

Aunt Beth: Every one of your paternal aunts is very different, but Beth is the most different. She was always a difficult child and always seeking this idyllic vision of what our family should be like. She's bitter that we moved away and wanted to live our own lives. She doesn't remember that our family get-togethers were never conflict-free. Hopefully someday she'll realize the way our family really is rather than dreaming about the way our family should be.

Uncle Jed: My brother and I were not particularly close as kids. He was much more athletic, tough and adventuresome than me. He was truly his father's son. He has, in the last several years, really matured and although we'll likely never be close, I like him.

Tony DiCioccio: Tony and I have been good or best friends since sophomore year of high school. We rented cottages in Harwichport for two weeks each summer after our junior and senior years of high school. In college, we used to have long talks about everything. He's the first person I've ever known that can relate to anyone—a teenage rockstar or a bank president. I think that he'll be a good godfather for you although he'll probably spoil you.

Well, that's about it for now. I won't tell you about the current state of affairs in the world as I'm leaving you some newspapers and magazines. I will say, however, that I dread the thought of George Bush and Dan Quayle being elected. Bush is a nice guy but is too passive to be an effective president. Quayle is just a rich kid who is totally unqualified to lead this country.

I hope you've had a good life so far and that things only get better. Remember that no matter whatever happens over the next 18 years, your mother and I love you.

Love,
Dad

chapter six
i just go

Moulin Rouge is our soundtrack for life. I pinky promise you he sings "Your Song" better than Ewan McGregor; we did our own rendition of "Elephant Love Medley" more than once down the halls of Jesuit. Random bands are our obsession. It's a race to see who can find perfect music before the other, and we usually both win because we stalk completely different music scenes. For my inca-pable-of-sleep self, it's all about the indy-acoustic guitar. For crazy scene-kid him, it's all about screamo and punk.

-Megan McAninch

Music was always an important part of our family. It was used to inspire and to entertain. It became part of memorable events. It could trigger wholesale memories. We used music to bond ourselves as a family. We used music to woo and to soothe, to excite and to dance, and to comfort and console. We created our own songs and copied others.

I grew up playing music, whether piano, drums or guitar, and lis-tening to a wide range of musical styles. My father played saxophone in local bands when he was younger and, again, when he retired. My brother was an accomplished musician and I was, at best, someone who enjoyed playing music even if I couldn't play it well. I consider myself a musician as much as I consider myself an athlete. I consider myself an athlete only to the extent defined for me by a doctor who once treated me for a partial tear of my Achilles tendon.

Andy Mendenhall was a bit younger than me but a great physician. He explained that this condition was a very common injury for athletes like me.

I demurred and told him that I certainly wasn't an athlete. "Kevin," he told me, "Given how much you work out, you are an athlete…not a good athlete, of course, but still an athlete." I chuckled and accepted the backhanded compliment. Accordingly, I now consider myself both a musician and an athlete—but neither a good musician nor a good athlete.

Being the youngest of six children, I was introduced to different musical styles and artists by my older siblings, as well as my father. My sisters exposed me to everything from Motown to folk music, and my brother introduced me to country rock and heavy metal. Of course my brother also used to beat the crap out of me in a misguided attempt to toughen me up, but that is a story for another day.

My father introduced me to Tommy Dorsey, Duke Ellington, Frank Sinatra, and many others. There were many Saturday nights when I would come home late to find my dad listening to Big Band jazz on his reel-to-reel tape recorder. He would wave me over, saying, "Kid! Kid! Come over here. Listen to this horn section."

The mixture of scotch and cigarettes on his breath did nothing to diminish my understanding of his complete appreciation for a particularly exquisite musical arrangement. He would wag his finger, akin to a conductor waiving his baton, leading the horn section through some wondrous passage. My loving wife still mocks me to this day as I do the exact same thing.

In high school, my friends and I loved to introduce each other to new artists and songs. We bought eight-track recorders so that we could make our own eight-track tapes. We would sit in Tony DiCioccio's car and listen to Edgar Winter's *Frankenstein* on his quadraphonic car stereo. We "discovered" Alice Cooper and David Bowie. We were among the first in our little group at school to come to appreciate the Charlie Daniels Band and Poco. Led Zepplin and Eric Clapton were staples. James Taylor and Jethro Tull always seemed to be playing somewhere.

In college, I found a peculiar way to use music to relieve my teenage angst. Like most teenagers, I could feel the weight of the world on my shoulders and suffered from occasional bouts of depression. Back then, a breakup with a girl or a bad grade on a test seemed so import-ant and had an immense impact upon my psyche. Sometimes it just became too much. I discovered that when I was staring into that black hole of depression, the best thing to do was to embrace it, to allow the depression to envelop me—to "go dark." I would sit alone in a gloomy, dark room and listen to depressing music. For me it was usually James Taylor, although Jackson Browne did the trick also. As I focused on the soul-crushing lyrics of lost love and misery, I would wallow in self-pity.

Listening to tales of heartbreak and woe only works for so long and then becomes uninteresting and even boring. At that point, I would emerge from my dark solitude and embrace the world again. It rarely took more than thirty minutes or so for the boredom to overcome the angst. This process worked surprisingly well for a number of years and was an activity that I revisited in the weeks, months, and years after Conner's death.

* * *

With the arrival of Conner and Moira and my acceptance of my role as *paterfamilias*, I felt it was my duty to pass on a musical education to my children. When Conner was born, Raffi quickly became a staple of our household. We would sing "Brown Girl in the Rain" and "Apples and Bananas" over and over (and over) again. We also had a series of videos called *Wee Sing* that involved loose narratives with colorful char-acters and catchy tunes. We would always sing along with the videos and sometimes without them. Ours was a house filled with music and singing and laughter.

One of Conner's favorite songs was an old calypso song that I in-troduced him to, as performed by Arlo Guthrie. I would sing "Guabi Guabi" to him while he was a newborn and holding him in my arms. I taught him the words, which were a combination of Pidgin English and nonsense words, and we sang it loudly and proudly, if not well, through-out his early years.

When Moira arrived, she quickly absorbed the same musical education and, as an entire family, we sang the various ditties whether driving somewhere or just setting the table for dinner.

I also began to write songs for the kids. I wrote a theme song for each child that we would sing to wake them up in the morning or just to embarrass them when friends were around. I wrote songs to sing on the way to daycare or at bedtime. I even wrote bathroom songs. You haven't truly lived until you've sung "I've Got Nuggies in my Huggies" while nature is expressing an urgent need. I wrote a special, and incredibly silly, little chant that I recited every night for Moira as I put her to bed in order to keep the scary monsters at bay. I assumed accents and characters, becoming The Nakifer and The Bathinator when it was bath time.

I introduced both Conner and Moira to James Taylor and The Beatles. I introduced them to Steely Dan and Def Leppard. I introduced them to Willie Nelson, Collective Soul, William Topley, and Jonatha Brooke. Every time that I "discovered" a new artist, I felt compelled to introduce the artist to the kids. They, in turn, began to take great joy in introducing me to their "discoveries."

Conner called me into his room one evening to have me watch a video of Idina Menzel singing "For Good" from the Broadway show *Wicked*. I remember the sheer awe in his eyes as he watched her sing; amazed at the strength and range of her voice. As he got older, his musical tastes seemed to focus more on "screamo-rock" but he could appreciate all types of music, including Broadway show tunes. He loved *Moulin Rouge*. He loved *Godspell*. Moira introduced me to Alexi Murdoch, The Band Perry, and countless other artists. Conner introduced me, or at least tried to introduce me, to bands such as A Change of Pace and Scary Kids Scaring Kids. While I appreciated the musicianship, I didn't quite fit their target demographic.

* * *

My buddy Tony DiCioccio got into the music business after college. He initially worked as a merchandise accountant and then a tour accountant for various artists. Eventually, he moved into managing various artists. One time when Conner was about five years old, Tony was negotiating a merchandise deal for Judas Priest. The vendor brought by some letterman jackets that had leather sleeves and heavy wool with the band's insignia sewed on. It was a very elaborate and expensive jacket. Tony asked them if he could see the jacket in a child's size as he wanted to buy one for his godson. The vendor explained that they didn't make them in children's sizes. Tony again asked if he could see the jacket in the child's size and then just stared at the vendor and waited. That is how Conner ended up with a great Judas Priest jacket when he was only five years old. Of course, we rarely let him wear it, out of fear that it would be stolen, but we proudly displayed it around the house.

When Conner was about twelve years old, Tony came for a visit and we were driving somewhere with Jane, Conner, and Moira in the backseat. As we were talking about music, I looked back and asked Conner what his favorite type of music was. Obviously trying to impress Tony with the learned nature of his musical tastes, he perked up and proudly said, "Roxy Music."

Tony and I just looked at one another and began grinning. I looked at Conner in the rearview mirror and said, "You do know, don't you, that Roxy Music is the name of a band and not a style of music."

He looked at me for a second, then averted his eyes and, with an embarrassed grin, just said, "Oh."

* * *

Conner was almost three years old when Jane and I decided to pull a prank on my parents who were in town for a visit. We got a temporary tattoo of Metallica and put it on his butt. Then we showed it to my parents and told them that it was a real tattoo and that we did it for the cover of Metallica's next album. My parents, especially my father, were somewhat skeptical but we explained that Conner was getting paid

$40,000, which would be put into his college fund, and that this had all been arranged through Tony. They knew and trusted Tony so they accepted the general idea. As we were still discussing this, a news story about Metallica came on the TV that was playing in the background. In reality, the story was about a CD release party that Metallica was having in New York. My folks, however, only heard a reference to Metallica and they asked what the story was about.

With a completely straight face, I told them that the news story was that Metallica just filed for bankruptcy. My father looked at me and said, "Please tell me that you got Conner's money up front." I looked at him sheepishly, averted my eyes, and muttered "no" before finally erupting in laughter.

That was one of the few pranks that I was actually able to pull on the original Old Man.

* * *

More than just enjoying music, Conner loved the whole lifestyle. He would reach out to up-and-coming bands and help promote them locally. One band he met and befriended was A Change of Pace ("ACOP") out of the Phoenix area. He had stumbled upon the band through Myspace and reached out to one of the band members, Johnny Abdullah, and introduced himself. That began a long friendship between Conner and Johnny.

When the band made its first foray into the Northwest, Conner went to the show and helped. Thereafter, it was a little disconcerting, but not unusual, to get up on a Saturday or Sunday morning and find five or six guys sprawled out asleep in the living room. ACOP may have been the first, but certainly wasn't the last, struggling band to spend the night at our house. Without exception, the kids were unfailingly polite. I'm not sure if Conner was prouder to show the band off to his family or show his family off to the band.

Conner spent a summer after he graduated from high school working at the Sleep Country Amphitheater in Ridgefield, Washington. The hours were long and the work could be monotonous, but he loved it. He helped with marketing and just loved being around the music. He called his mother one time to tell her that he was having his lunch and listening to the Goo Goo Dolls perform its sound check. He was in seventh heaven.

When John Mayer came to town that summer, Conner got to meet him. Apparently, Mayer had a rather odd process of exploring a venue before he went on stage. He would don a bear costume and walk around the venue. People who saw had no idea who he was, so Mayer could wander about without being mobbed. Conner figured it out pretty quickly and asked to have a picture taken with him. I still have a great, albeit grainy, picture of a beaming Conner alongside John Mayer in his bear costume.

* * *

I found a great deal of solace in music after Conner's death. There were certain songs that just seemed to resonate with me when grief began to overwhelm me—when I would go dark. A few days after the accident, as I was pulling into the parking lot of the crematorium to pick up Conner's ashes, a song by Boz Scaggs came on. The song is titled "I Just Go" and the lyrics are as follows:

> *Don't know why I wandered off last night*
> *I was having a good time and feeling alright*
> *Feeling right at home with you*
> *Guess I hadn't had enough though of something*
> *And I just go.*
>
> *Saw some of my old running boys over by the back door*
> *Having a laugh thought I'd say hello and anyway*
> *Then one thing leads to another I guess*
> *I just go.*

I didn't realize till you left word for me
Your concern about where I'd disappeared to
And it never crossed my mind
That I'd worried you or been unkind in doing so

And I'm so, so sorry I took off so fast
That you felt abandoned and left out like that
Please understand
You see I just don't pay much mind sometimes
Sometimes I just go

I need you to know
How I long to do all you want me to
I'd go anywhere at all any time you call
To comfort you

And I take every word of your advice
I'd make any kind of sacrifice to let you know
But there's this other voice calling me sometimes
And I just go

© Boz Scaggs

It felt to me as if Conner was speaking to me through the song, as if he was reaching out to me. While it was Boz Scaggs' voice, it seemed to be Conner's spirit talking to me. It was as if he called up the song on my iPod at just that moment. The song hit me so hard that I just sat in the car and listened and cried. When the song was over, I played it again… and again. Finally, wiping away the tears, I walked inside and picked up Conner's ashes.

Over the following months, I found a number of other songs that seemed to resonate with my grief. "Inconsolable" by Jonatha Brooke and "One Moment More" and "Hurricane," both by Mindy Smith, remain favorites when I need to give in to the grief—when I need to go dark. The artists sing with an emotion that allows the darkness to consume and envelop me. Sometimes it is the lyrics but more often it is a combination of the lyrics and the artist's voice that seem to focus my despair. Sometimes it is the mournfulness of a guitar solo. The songs say, much more artfully than I ever could, what I am feeling at that moment. They express the anguish in a way that is compelling and welcome. They allow me to experience the depth and pain of shared grief.

Sometimes I need to feel the pain. Sometimes I need to experience the heartache. Knowing that I will never talk with my son again or give him a hug, I need to experience the physical sensations involved with the grief. The pain helps me to keep him alive in my heart. As long as I feel the pain from his death, Conner is still with me. In the pain I find solace and, at least for a while, my grief and guilt are overwhelmed rather than being overwhelming. When it is just me and the music, I allow myself to truly grieve. I allow myself to remember. I allow myself to cry.

chapter seven

busy

I am tired of the pain my heart feels every time you cross my mind. The tears that come to my eyes when I hear a song that reminds me of you are so hard to fight back. I don't understand why you are gone. I don't think I ever will. Your dad said it so well in your eulogy. And I do believe you filled your purpose. Yet, I want to be selfish. I cannot stand to see so many people around me so broken. And it just does not seem real to me at all.

One day we will meet again. I wish I didn't have to say goodbye to someone who kept life interesting. When I start to cry, like I am right now, I try so hard to focus on the fact that you are looking over me and protecting me. Then I get angry because I don't want to accept it. I'm in a constant battle with my emotions. Never again can I hear "FAIL!" or "That's what she said!" without thinking of you. I miss and love you ConCon.

-Macky Maruhn

While we understood the pace of progress and how the world seemed to have shrunk thanks to constant technological advances, we were still amazed at how quickly the news of Conner's death spread. The television stations reported the accident but hadn't yet identified him. It was through the social media sites like Facebook, as well as telephones and texting, that people learned of his death.

While Jane and I continued to make and receive phone calls throughout that first morning, people started coming over. Friends brought food and just wanted to be around us. For so many, our house had been a place of joy and laughter, and people weren't ready to give that up yet. The fact that it was a glorious sunny Saturday was a point of irony. The house was quickly filled with friends and family, as well as with noise and the smell of cooking food. At one point, one of the neighborhood kids came by to express his sympathies. Reid and Conner had been friends in grade school and middle school but hadn't seen much of each other in the prior six years. He brought some flowers and gave us each a hug. We were so impressed by his maturity and empathy.

The fact that we were surrounded by so many friends kept us busy, too busy to really dwell upon what had happened. One group was in the kitchen cooking; others were in the backyard drinking and telling stories; others repeatedly ran to the store for more groceries and drinks. Some just sat quietly, not sure what to say but wanting to be there for us. Anyone who wanted to talk about Conner was welcomed. We wanted to hear stories.

Shortly before noon, I met with the Deputy Medical Examiner who had first broken the news to Moira. He brought by some personal effects that had been recovered from the car. Included in this little white plastic bag were my checkbook, the garage door opener, a photo album, and a couple of miscellaneous pieces of paper.

That was it.

That was all that could be recovered from the crash site.

At that point, my knowledge of the accident was very sketchy, and he was able to provide a little bit more information. He explained that the initial investigation found that Conner was driving northbound through a construction zone on I-5 at about 2:15 a.m. when he ran into the back of an asphalt carrier. The truck had been working in the center median and was pulling into the far right lane when the impact occurred.

The collision was sufficiently violent that he was killed instantly. The car, my Saab 9-3 convertible, spun around after the impact, flipped, and burst into flames. The driver of the truck, together with the driver of a passing vehicle, tried to put out the fire and succeeded initially.

Unfortunately, the car reignited and burned until it eventually burned itself out.

The Deputy Medical Examiner explained that the fires had horribly burned Conner's body, but that they were able to see four stars tattooed on his chest. These tattoos, which he had gotten on his 18th birthday, allowed the identification of his body.

With only this little bit of sketchy information and with an overwhelming sense of loss, I assumed that the truck driver was responsible. I was certain that he had somehow made too rapid a lane change and/or had not had his lights properly on and working. I became convinced that he had, in fact, cut Conner off. I was angry. The anger was like a smoldering ember. This wasn't the time or place to explode but it smoldered. I blamed the driver for my son's death. I began planning how we would sue him. I knew which attorney I would hire. I wanted the driver to pay for his carelessness. I wanted him to pay for my son's death. It wasn't a money thing. I wanted to hold him responsible for my son's death. I wanted to face him and have a jury condemn him. I wanted an explanation but, more importantly, I wanted someone to blame. I wanted justice.

I went through numerous scenarios to explain the accident, none of which involved any fault on the part of Conner. This mental exercise distracted me and allowed me to continue to keep a small measure of my grief at bay, at least for short periods of time.

Early in the afternoon, we decided that it was time to drive by the accident site. We knew the approximate area of the accident but still had too few details. We finally found the site in the breakdown lane. Scorched asphalt and bits and pieces of the Saab strewn on the side of the road marked the spot. We found a small piece of tire tread and months later had it made into a bracelet for Jane. We found a small piece of the bumper and gave it to Moira as a memento. I kept the spare key to the Saab. I keep that key in the glove box of my car. I get some odd comfort by just holding the key. It has become a talisman that allows me to feel closer to Conner and to times long since gone.

After finding the accident site, Jane insisted that we go to the morgue and see Conner. She wanted to be absolutely sure that it was him. A part of her still believed that this was just some grotesque mistake. I refused. I knew that the impact and the fires had charred and disfigured Conner's body. There was no way that I wanted Jane to have to live with that image of our son. We both needed to remember him as we did, as our handsome and happy boy. She reluctantly agreed, likely because she was just too exhausted, both emotionally and physically, to argue about it.

Shortly after returning home, the head of campus ministry at Jesuit High School came by. With his assistance, we planned a prayer vigil for the following evening, Sunday night, at the school and then a memorial mass on Tuesday night.

Throughout the rest of the day, people came and went. We comforted more than we were comforted, although we certainly found great comfort in the waves of compassion and friendship that we experienced that day. Gradually, people started to drift away as night fell and then it was just the three of us. We sat quietly in the living room, the silence of the house deafening. We spoke of the days to come: the prayer vigil and memorial mass. We talked about the family members and out-of-town friends that would be arriving the next day. We deftly danced around the reason why we were going through this, instinctively knowing that it wasn't time to talk about that yet. So we simply said goodnight and went upstairs to bed. Both Jane and I gave Moira extra long hugs as we walked her to her room. We told her how much we loved her and that everything would be all right. We all knew that it was an empty assurance but one that we needed to make nonetheless. At that point in time, I didn't believe that everything would ever be all right again.

Jane and I lay next to each other in bed, our hands clasped tightly under a light blanket, with the dog lying at our feet. We were too tired to sleep but too afraid to say anything for fear that one or both of us might crack and be unable to recover. I could hear Jane's breathing slow as she gradually fell asleep.

I lay there and watched the clock, dreading the approaching midnight hour. As difficult as that day, September 12, 2009, had been, as emotionally devastating as it had been, it was still the last day that Conner was alive. It was the last day that he and I had breathed the same air. It was the last day that I had a living son. Once midnight came and a new day began, it would be the first day *after.* It would be our first day, our first full day, without Conner or, more accurately, the first full day with nothing but memories of Conner. It would be the first day of a new life, one that would be wholly different yet achingly familiar. I didn't want the day to end but, of course, it did. It had to.

chapter eight
bobbyman

It was my day off and I was sleeping when I got a text from Moira: "Hey, are you awake?" Immediately I thought Moira had gotten into trouble somehow and that she needed me to do something for her or that maybe Conner screwed up somehow and needed my help. I'm half asleep and just wanted to fall back asleep so I texted back, "I'm at work." I was just trying to get out of it, whatever "it" was. Total dick move!

She then texted back and just told me – flat out. "Conner is dead." I thought I was having a heart attack. Literally, I thought I was having a heart attack at that moment when I read that text.

I jumped up, threw on whatever clothes were closest and went over to the Lubys'. I called as many people as I could on the drive over. I got through to my Mom, Jeff, Matt, and I think one other person.

The thought that I lied to Moira, just as she was trying to tell me about Conner, made me feel really guilty. That just broke my heart.

-Jonathon Pelzner

I t's funny how things turn out sometimes. I was working for a medium-sized law firm at the time Conner was born. A month later, right before Thanksgiving, I was laid off. The firm had just lost its major client and, scrambling to remain viable, decided to make some cuts. I was expendable and quickly realized how poorly I had understood and played the game of office politics. I naively believed that I was something other than an easily replaceable, not even wholly necessary, cog in the machine.

Obviously, it was stressful to try and figure out how to support a family of three on unemployment, especially around the holidays, but I was certain that my next job was just around the corner. The fact that it took me six months to find that next job was actually a blessing, albeit sometimes in a very depressing disguise and not truly appreciated until years later. During this time, I was Conner's primary caregiver. Jane was working so I was the one caring for him during the day.

Being so young, Conner was pretty easy to care for at this time. Like all newborns, he slept a lot and, when he wasn't sleeping, he was eating and/or messing his diapers. While I was, of course, anxious to find a new job, I was still able to find the time to sit on the couch and just hold him. I remember staring into his face and trying to imagine what he would look like in one, five—and even ten—years. I would consider his future and wonder if he would be an athlete or a scholar or musician. I tried to unlock the secrets of his future with absolutely no success. It was remarkable, however, that it felt so comfortable to cradle him in my arms. Despite the financial stress of unemployment, I got to experience a measure of contentedness just by holding him and hearing him breathe.

We placed a small basketball hoop on the back of his door and, when I had nothing better to do (which was much of the time), I would hold him in one arm while playing imaginary games of basketball with the other. I would have him hold the ball and lift him up so that he could dunk it. Obviously, at that age, he had no idea what he was doing but I mimicked crowds cheering for him with every dunk. He became the star of our personal little fantasy basketball league.

I was remarkably adept at holding him in my left arm and doing everything else—from eating, to writing, to changing channels—with my right. It just felt comfortable and natural to hold him. I was a dad and very proud of that role.

I still remember Conner waking up one time in the middle of the night. Jane had to work the next day so it was my turn to get up. He wasn't dirty and he wasn't hungry. He was just awake and bored. Perhaps I should have recognized that this was a harbinger of what was to come. In any event, it was about 2:00 a.m. and I held him in my arms and just walked back and forth in his room for almost an hour. I sang softly and every time I laid him down, thinking that he had fallen asleep, he would open his eyes and cry again. Conner needed to be held and, despite the fact that I was practically walking in my sleep, I did so with no rancor or aggravation. He was a gift and I loved the fact that my son found comfort in his father's arms. Okay, if truth be told, I can't say for sure that there wasn't *any* rancor or aggravation at the time but, certainly in hindsight, there was none of any lasting note.

* * *

As most new parents discover, friendships change when you are the first of your friends to become parents. We brought Conner with us almost wherever we went. If we went to dinner, Conner was in his carrier. If we went hiking, Conner was in the backpack. If we went to the beach, we brought Conner and all of his supplies with us. He might have slept through most of it, but we were adamant that we wanted to maintain our active lifestyle and we wanted him to be exposed to, and become accustomed to, an active lifestyle. It didn't always work with other couples, especially those who were childless, and many of those couples slowly drifted out of our lives. Fortunately, we developed new friendships with other parents and the friends lost were replaced.

Eventually, I went back to work but that job, for various reasons, was relatively short-lived, lasting only about seven months. Once again, I found myself as Conner's primary caregiver shortly after he turned one. This stint only lasted four months, but it was certainly more challenging as Conner was much more mobile and highly energetic. At times when I just needed to wear him out, I would take him to the airport. A wide tunnel led to the parking garage. It was carpeted, well lit and very wide and very long. I would have him just run and run (or, more accurately, waddle and waddle) until he was exhausted. We would laugh and chase one another. I would challenge him to run to the end of the tunnel (over a hundred yards) and then run back. He always accepted the challenge. Even then I recognized his desire to please me.

Afterwards, we would drive to the end of the airport runway and watch the planes take off and land. His eyes would fill with awe as he watched these huge planes fly overhead, and then his eyelids would begin to flutter and he would gently fall asleep from exhaustion. It was one of the greatest times of my life.

* * *

One of the little tricks we played on Conner at this age involved candy, or at least what he thought was candy. Certainly he had heard about candy. He'd seen the advertisements on television and at the movies; he had been around older kids who ate candy. Heck, he probably even saw his mother (but never me!) eating it. We, of course, didn't want him developing a sugar habit at too young of an age so we came up with an idea. We bought frozen mixed vegetables—a combination of carrots, peas, and green beans cut into small pieces. We would serve these colorful and chilly treats to him as a dessert and tell him that it was candy. He thought that was great…until he found out the truth.

* * *

While many kids have a special toy or stuffed animal that brings them comfort, Conner had his security blanket. He named the blanket "Bobby." It was a simple white child's blanket with satin edging. He loved that damn thing. He slept with it and carried it around the house with him at all times. Wherever he went, Bobby was there. If we went out, Bobby came with us. Whether in the car or just a stroller, Bobby was always there. One night we used a new babysitter so that Jane and I could have a date night. When we came home, the poor girl was beside herself because Conner started crying for "Bobby." She had no idea that Bobby wasn't a "he" but, rather, an "it" and she had no way of comforting him. We had made the mistake of washing Bobby and not taking him out of the dryer before we left. As this was before the advent of cell phones, she was unable to contact us. Conner eventually cried himself to sleep. The babysitter subsequently declined our requests to return and sit for him again.

Jane was smart enough to figure out that the way to avoid future incidents like that was to buy extra "Bobbies." We kept an extra Bobby in the car. We kept an extra Bobby in his diaper bag. We kept an extra Bobby hidden in a dresser drawer for washday. Bobby would never come up missing again.

I taught Conner that by loosely tying Bobby around his neck, he could fashion a cape and turn himself into a superhero. He would wear his jammies, put on knee high socks, tie on his Bobby cape, and grab a sword. He would then run through the house, fighting villains, righting wrongs, and generally wreaking havoc. We called this character "Bobbyman."

Often I would join him and find ways to dress up as a pirate or oddly-dressed superhero to accompany Bobbyman on his adventures. One evening, I stripped off all of my clothes, fashioned a bandanna and a belt to serve as my loincloth, turned one of my ties into a flowing headband, and grabbed a Nerf archery set from Conner's room. He put on his Bobbyman costume and we began to stalk Jane throughout the house. We would leap out from behind the couch, or behind a door, and chase her around and around. The poor woman never stood a chance.

I wrote the following poem for Conner and his alter ego:

BOBBYMAN
by Kevin W. Luby

When lives are in danger,
When no one else can,
They cry out for help,
They cry for...BOBBYMAN!

When the dam is a-bursting,
When the crap hits the fan,
Who comes to the rescue?
Why it's...BOBBYMAN!

When the world's run amuck,
When they can't form a plan,
They look to the skies,
They look to...BOBBYMAN!

When catastrophe calls,
When they all need a hand,
They reach out in hope,
They reach to...BOBBYMAN!

When they get terribly sunburned,
When they just wanted a tan,
They scream out in anguish,
They scream for...BOBBYMAN!

And it was good.

* * *

In the middle of winter, we wore slippers or socks as the floors, and particularly the tile on the bathroom floor, got very cold. One night I was getting Conner ready for his bath. As he was standing naked next to the bathtub and watching the tub fill with water, I decided to challenge him. I told him that I didn't think that he could lie down on the cold tile floor for thirty seconds—buck naked. He grinned and promptly lay down. He squirmed and squealed but stayed there the full time.

Jane was watching and listening to all this from the kitchen, and she decided that my challenge wasn't quite fair. Accordingly, she came into the bathroom and suggested, with one of the most evil smirks that I have ever seen, that I should also lie down on the cold tile floor, also buck naked, and see if I could also stay there for thirty seconds. With Conner pretty much staring me down, I stripped down and lay there on that cold, cold tile floor. Both Conner and Jane thought this was hysterical and I realized, not for the last time, that Jane and Conner enjoyed a particularly special bond and would not hesitate to gang up on me.

* * *

Conner and I created our own form of roughhousing. We called it "having kapowee talks." Like professional wrestling, we would pretend to hit one another, yelling, "kapowee!"; then the other would flop down onto the ground or the bed writhing in pretend pain. Conner was inexhaustible in this game. The only hesitation that Jane ever had is that I sometimes started these kapowee talks right before bedtime. I thought it would tucker him out. Jane thought it would wind him up. Jane was right and I was wrong, but that never really stopped us from doing it. It was just too much fun.

* * *

Perhaps partly because he was a high-energy child, he was a very sloppy eater. He had to do everything quickly and that included inhaling his food. Even when we were still spoon-feeding him in his highchair, he would manage to get his hands into the cereal and then run them through his hair. Jane started saying that he was so dirty, gooey and sticky that he was...*mookie*! Hence, Conner got his first nickname. For the rest of his life, Jane would refer to him as "Mookie" and "Mookie Boy." Over the years I would shorten it to "Moo" or "Moo Moo."

One variation of this nickname became "Moishe." I'm not sure when or where this started but it did. This nickname then served as my inspiration for an epic poem that I wrote for Conner entitled, "Moishe, Desert Warrior." We all loved Shel Silverstein and I was writing short poems of the same genre. They were offbeat but I took great pride in coming up with them and Conner, and later Moira, loved them.

Once I started feeling comfortable with shorter, humorous poems, I decided to take a stab at a lengthier poem. It was, of course, written for Conner and a new fictional alter ego—Moishe. I used to recite it to Conner, using dramatic voices throughout. Jane would join in on the first two and last two stanzas as a sort of Greek chorus. He would sit and listen, absolutely beaming throughout the recitation.

As he got older, the poem began to embarrass him which, of course, only made it more fun for Jane and me. We threatened to recite it around friends and he would be horrified. Even into his teen years, Jane and I would, from time to time, break out and recite the first two stanzas. Despite his obvious embarrassment, I know he was proud of the fact that his dad wrote an epic poem just for him.

MOISHE, DESERT WARRIOR
By Kevin W. Luby

Moishe, Desert Warrior,
Flies across the sand,
Fighting evil and injustice,
All throughout the land.

A doer of good deeds,
A hero, brave and strong,
A friend to all good people,
Who makes right every wrong.

There came one stormy morning,
Some bad news from the East,
Of a cruel and evil tyrant,
Some even called this man a beast.

Biknar was his name,
And he caused oh, such a fright,
By creating mayhem by day,
And shear terror every night.

He would lie and he would cheat,
He would hurt and he would steal,
He would take all of your money,
And he would eat all your last meal.

So to Moishe this day came,
A bruised and battered man,
"My name, Moishe, is Andrew,
Please rid Biknar from my land."

"He tortures and he hurts us,
And he drives away the sun,
There is no one else to help us,
I know you're the only one."

Brave Moishe listened well,
And to himself he thought,
I must go right away,

There's a battle to be fought.

He quickly gathered his belongings,
And jumped upon his horse,
Waved goodbye to all his friends,
And set off on his course.

He traveled many days,
Under a fierce and brutal sun,
Heading for Biknar's castle,
The home of the Evil One.

Moishe saw many travelers,
And heard so many tales,
Of others, against Biknar,
Who had battled and had failed.

Biknar's strength was legend,
And his power...it was vast,
Moishe could easily understand,
How others had failed so in the past.

But undaunted, yes he was,
Moishe would never think to quit,
If he couldn't match Biknar with strength,
He would have to best Biknar with wit.

Oh! And there, upon a distant ridge,
Moishe finally spied,
The castle of the Evil One,
The end of Moishe's ride.

But just then it got much darker,

As Moishe began to draw near,
A nasty trick by Biknar,
To spread both terror and fear.

Oh, yes, and circling high up above,
And slithering on the earth below,
Were Biknar's evil creatures,
Putting on quite a show.

They had horns and they had fangs,
They had sharp and ugly claws,
And they sneered and they growled,
With slime dripping from their jaws.

But brave Moishe stood tall in his saddle,
And fixed them all a stare,
And they wouldn't look him in the eye,
None would even dare.

'cause Moishe was true and he was brave,
As he called out with a song,
"Go away you evil creatures,
Go away now and be gone!"

And they scattered, yes they did,
They left ever so fast,
They cleared all away,
And let brave Moishe go past.

And then Moishe reached the castle,
It was made of thick iron plate,
He got up off his horse,
And knocked upon the gate.

Well, the gate so quickly opened,
It made a horrible crash,
It sounded much like thunder,
With a sharp lightning-like flash.

The wind began wildly whipping,
The dust into the air,
But Brave Moishe stood his ground,
And waited for his vision to clear.

And when it finally did,
Not a hundred feet away,
Was a terrible sight to see,
Who loudly called out to say...

"Who has come to my castle?
Who has vanquished my beasts?
Who has come to my home,
Where his life will soon cease?"

Moishe just stared straight at Biknar,
Without saying a single word.
He checked out his foe,
And the words he had heard.

For Biknar was larger than huge,
And he was taller than tall,
He was so massive a man,
It was hard to imagine at all.

He had a sword in one hand,
And an axe in the other,

And his face was so ugly,
You had to pity his mother.

Now Moishe knew in his heart,
Based on strength alone, he would lose,
But he knew he must win,
So his words he carefully choosed.

"I come bearing a present,
And Moishe's my name,"
He said with a smile,
While Biknar stared just the same.

"Who needs silly gifts?"
Biknar said, "I own,
All that I see,
Now just leave me alone."

Moishe said, "I have gold and jewels,
Much too heavy to bear,
And I keep them well hidden,
Not too far from here."

"Though rich that I am,
You would never detect it,
For people would steal it from me,
So I need you to protect it."

"I offer a deal,
I'll give you one-half my cash,
If you'll agree to protect me,
And the rest of my stash."

Well, a glimmer seemed to light,
In both of Biknar's eyes,
And the corners of his mouth,
Well, they started to rise.

"A great sum of riches, you say,
Not too far from here?
All I need do is protect you,
On that, am I clear?"

Moishe said, "You're the strongest by far,
You're feared throughout the land,
My wealth would be well-protected,
As best that it can."

"Well, my friend," Biknar said,
"I think we have a deal.
On me you can depend,
For my promise is real."

So Moishe led the way,
As Biknar brought up the rear.
"With me," Biknar hissed,
"You now have nothing to fear."

And into the hills they went,
To the mountains they rode,
If either got tired,
It never showed.

And just before dark,
They stopped by a deep cave,
"This is it," Moishe said,

"Where I've hid all that I've saved."

"For deep in this cave,
Are my riches galore,
All one could ask for,
And even much more!"

Suddenly, Biknar grabbed Moishe,
And held him high in the air,
"How foolish, little Moishe,
To think I'd want to share."

"We had a firm deal,
So now how can you say..."
But Biknar just laughed,
And tossed Moishe away.

Laughing he ran,
Far, far into the cave,
Looking to steal,
All poor Moishe had saved.

But after several minutes,
There came such a roar,
"There's nothing of value here,
What did you bring me here for?"

Moishe yelled, "There's water aplenty,
And good books to read,
There's also some fresh food,
That's all that you'll need."

And with that smart Moishe,

Kicked loose a stone,
And started the avalanche,
That sealed Biknar's new home.

Brave Moishe had won,
But not by strength, size or speed,
You see, Biknar was defeated,
By his own treachery and greed.

Well with Biknar now gone,
And his creatures cast out,
The people rejoiced,
They sang with a shout...

Moishe, Desert Warrior,
Flies across the sand,
Fighting evil and injustice,
All throughout the land.

A doer of good deeds,
A hero brave and strong,
A friend to all good people,
Who makes right every wrong.

I can still clearly remember lying down next to Conner on his "big boy" bed, as he was just starting to fall asleep, and softly, but dramatically, reciting this poem to him, night after night. He was my Moishe, my Mookie Boy, my Moo Moo.

When I got a tattoo on my forearm after his death, a part of it—below the Celtic knot and the dates of his birth and death—says "Moo2."

* * *

With my return to full-time employment, daycare became a necessity. We fumbled through a number of different providers, smartly avoiding the couple that kept their collection of pit bulls in a kennel just outside the children's play area. We finally came upon a woman who had recently quit her job with a law firm to take care of her daughter and wisely decided to set up a small daycare. Amy Cleary was a wonder, as were her helpers. They took on a small group of kids all about Conner's age. This was his first opportunity to make friends and he wasted no time in doing so. Conner, Morgan, Rory and Ben became close friends, as did their parents. It was safe and reliable and a great relief to Jane and me.

One evening I went to pick up Conner and Amy pulled me aside. She quietly told me that I needed to be more careful about my language as Conner was using some inappropriate language around the other kids. I asked what he was saying and she told me that he was starting to shout, "Fuck it! Damn it!" I looked at her for a moment and then started laughing. I raised my hands in mock horror and protested that it wasn't me. It turns out that my lovely and ever-so-innocent-looking wife was the one who needed to corral her mouth around young and impressionable ears. The truth was, the both of us have our moments where we curse like sailors. We just needed to make sure that we chose the appropriate time and place to embrace our profanity.

After a year or so at Amy's, she unexpectedly advised us that Conner was set to graduate. She explained that she had decided not to care for children over the age of three. Ultimately we figured out, that while she dearly loved Conner, he was a bit too rambunctious for her daycare. He was very energetic and the portion of her house that she used for the daycare just couldn't contain him. So off we went to a larger daycare—Children's Garden.

* * *

We took some time exploring various options and settled on Children's Garden because it was clean and well staffed. We liked the teachers and the facility and it was in a good location. I dropped Conner off on his first morning and went off to work. I returned about 10:00 a.m. to check in on him and walked into the large classroom. Two groups of kids sat on either side of the room being read to by the teachers. I went to the first group and the teacher directed me to the other group. I walked up to the second group and looked at the circle of children but didn't see Conner. I caught the teacher's eye and she nodded off to the side. There was Conner, in a fetal position and with his eyes closed, just sobbing. My heart broke.

I picked him up and hugged him. He was crying and saying he wanted to go back to Amy's. I held him in my arms and just comforted him. We ended up sitting on the floor with the second group, with him on my lap. I stayed for about an hour as the teacher told stories and interacted with the kids. Gradually, Conner began to participate and to talk with some of his new classmates. I was finally able to go back to work, and that was the last time I ever saw him insecure in a social situation.

* * *

Conner's confidence and social nature really blossomed after that initial day at Children's Garden. He became friends with a large number of his classmates, both boys and girls, and even at that young age seemed to have a particular affinity for talking to the pretty girls.

When we moved on to kindergarten, Conner had a male teacher—Gene Casquiero. Gene was a great teacher and was used to working with "busy" kids like Conner. Shortly before parent-teacher conferences, Gene had each child write down the name of his or her best friend in the class. Out of only thirty-two students, Conner was named fifteen times as "the" best friend. That's when we first knew that there was something truly special about him.

I also need to note that Conner as "the" best friend continued for the rest of his life. In interviewing people for this book, I listened to a myriad of people describe themselves as "Conner's best friend," or who described Conner as their best friend. The fact is that he *was* "best friends" with a large number of people, both male and female. At times in his life, it was Jon, other times Jeff, and other times Larry, Logan, Mike, or Nate. At times, it was Abbi or Ashley or Macky.

Conner had such a vast array of friends that his "best friend" depended on who he was with at the time and what he wanted to do.

The one friend who seemed to have the deepest friendship with Conner, however, was Megan McAninch. They met early in high school and in many ways were complete opposites. Megan was driven, cultured and well-traveled. She was involved in countless clubs and activities. She was steady as a rock. In other words, she was so many of the things that Conner was not. And yet they bonded.

They found common ground and influenced one another. It was a friendship that did not require give and take. Neither of them needed anything from the other; but both gave their hearts to one another. It wasn't a romantic love but, rather, the type of pure love found only in the deepest of friendships. There was no contemplation of romance, but there was the knowledge that beneath all of the trappings of ordinary life, they shared a common spirit and that they were bound to one another. Their respective assets and deficiencies complemented one another. They would always be there when the other needed someone to talk to or laugh with. They were kindred spirits, a fact perhaps only really understood by the two of them and their closest friends. They were friends of the truest sort.

* * *

We enjoyed the year with Mr. Casquiero so much that Conner and I wrote a short poem for him as a year-end gift.

ODE TO A KINDERGARTEN TEACHER
By Kevin W. Luby and Conner Luby

I think that I shall never see,
A teacher quite like Mr. C.
Tall of stature, good of looks,
He helped me start to read 'dem books!

With kind words, he was swell,
He even taught me how to spel.
While vexed a time or two, I fear,
He never yelled or kicked my rear.

Years from now, when I'm smart and
Thinking about kinder-gart-en,
As older people oft times do,
I'll look at his picture and wonder...
    "Mister Who?"

It was also in this kindergarten class where another family tradition began. As part of the parent-teacher conference, the parents were asked to write a short note to their child and leave it on his or her desk. We did so, of course, but rather than signing it with something as ordinary as "Mom and Dad," we signed it as "Colleen and Abdul."

The next day, Conner came home and asked who Colleen and Abdul were. With tongues planted firmly in our cheeks and with smiles upon our lips, we told Conner that he was adopted and that Colleen and Abdul were his real parents.

This was all part of how our family played tricks with and upon one another. Our tricks were warped and perhaps even ill-advised occasionally, but that was our family. Little was off-limits when it came to humor. Conner always understood that the concept of Colleen and Abdul was a joke. Nonetheless, we would thereafter refer to them as Conner's "real" parents whenever we wanted to tweak him or to come up with some excuse for saying "no" to one of his many requests. "Conner, we would buy you that mini-bike but Colleen and Abdul said no."

Of course, he would also use it if he thought we were being unduly strict or otherwise unreasonable. We heard on more than one occasion, "But Colleen and Abdul would let me…"

I should also mention that we continued this same tradition with Moira when she got old enough. Her imaginary birth parents, however, were named Buddy and Beatrice Tavares. Heaven forbid that we should suggest to our kids that they had the same pretend birth parents!

$$* * *$$

Having grown up during the Civil Rights era, it was always very important to us that Conner avoid racism. We employed, however, somewhat unorthodox ways of teaching him about racism.

One of Conner's first best friends was Larry Floyd. They had gone to pre-school together and then both families moved from Portland to Tigard. Larry was a year older but the boys ended up in a second/third grade class together and stayed together through middle school. One summer evening when the boys were in third or fourth grade, Conner came up and asked if he could invite Larry over for dinner. I calmly inquired, "Larry who?"

"Larry Floyd," he said, looking a bit puzzled.

I quickly and quietly, but emphatically, said, "Conner, no! Of course not!"

Conner looked up at me and said, "Dad, why not?"

I crouched down and put my hand on his shoulder. In a low, conspiratorial voice, I said, "Conner, Larry is…*black*!"

Conner stared at me for what seemed like ten seconds and then broke out in a knowing smirk and said, "You're such a jerk!" Needless to say, Larry came to dinner that evening and many evenings thereafter.

* * *

While parenting felt very natural to both Jane and me, it involved a lot of experimentation on our part. Many of our efforts succeeded and many of them failed, resulting in us having to backtrack. Sometimes we just took wild leaps of faith.

When we moved to Tigard, Conner was only seven years old. We bought a larger house in a nicer and safer neighborhood. There was a park nearby and sidewalks where Conner, and eventually Moira, could ride bikes.

Moira was only three at the time so she didn't mind the move but Conner was not so sure about this change. He was excited about the new neighborhood but missed the only home that he had had up to then. A couple of weeks after the move, Jane and I made the mistake of going back to the old house with Conner. The purpose of the visit was to talk to the new owner and let her know about some of the "quirks" of the house. Conner wanted to visit our old neighbors and see the house one last time.

The new owner welcomed us in and Conner quickly ran up to his old room. The new owner had a teenage son who, even in that short period of time, had not been kind to Conner's old room. We watched as Conner suddenly ran down the stairs, tears streaming, and raced out to the car. We bade the new owner goodbye and went out to the car to find out why Conner was so upset.

He was sobbing and kept saying that he wanted to go back to his old house and his old room. He hated the new house and just wanted everything the way it used to be. By the time we got home, he had stopped crying but was still upset and demanding that we move back "home."

I sat on the couch with my arm around him. "Conner, here's the deal," I told him. "We're going to stay here for the next two months. At that point, if you still want to move back to the old house, we will."

Talk about taking a risk! This promise calmed him down quickly. He looked as me. "Really?" he asked.

I looked at him, and then looked at Jane, who wore a look of stunned amazement at my audacity. I took a deep breath and assured him that this was a promise. Jane and I had numerous conversations over the following weeks, acknowledging that we would have some serious problems if Conner didn't grow to love the new house. Fortunately, the gamble paid off and it was only a matter of weeks before Conner had found new friends and discovered the joys of the new neighborhood. He never asked to move back.

In fact, at dinner on the two-month anniversary of my gambit, we told Conner that he now had to decide what we, as a family, should do. He promptly announced that we should stay where we were. We, of course, couldn't just leave that alone. Both Jane and I then began saying, "Gee, I don't know. The old house was really special." A panicked look briefly appeared in Conner's eyes until he realized that we were just teasing him and that we weren't, in fact, interested in living anywhere other than our new home.

* * *

It was only a few years later that we took a vacation on Cape Cod to visit friends and family. Conner was about twelve years old, tall and wiry. He had already far surpassed me as far as athletic ability was concerned. I may have been bigger and stronger than him, but it was just getting to the point where he was probably faster than me. And he had much better stamina than I did.

One day we were at the beach with an old high school friend and his family. Tom Garrahan and I had run cross-country and track for a couple of years and he had always been faster than me.

I came up with the idea to have the three of us race and both of them quickly agreed. Since I was arranging the race, I was in the middle. I placed Conner to my right, in about four inches of water. I placed Tom to my left, on the soft sand. I was standing on the hard-packed sand at the ocean's edge.

Before either of them could say anything about their placement, I said "Go!" Not surprisingly, I won the race. It took Tom months, and Conner years, to figure out the real reason that I won. I made sure, however, to never allow a rematch.

* * *

I was at a pre-season soccer coaches' meeting when my cell phone started to ring. I answered and it was Conner. He was upset and told me that mom had found a playing card with a naked woman on it and had blamed him. Despite his denial that it was his, she apparently didn't believe him. I explained to Conner that my meeting was almost over and that I would be home soon and we could straighten things out. I warned him, however, that when I got home, I was going to ask him what happened and that, whatever he told me, I would believe him because I knew that he would never lie to his father. He was not yet a teenager and this was another of my wild, and not particularly well-thought-out, gambits.

A few minutes later, I left the meeting and drove home. As I walked into the house, I could hear talking and, as I opened the door, Conner ran out of the kitchen. I looked at Jane and she was just standing there with her mouth agape. She explained to me that she had, in fact, found one of those old-fashioned playing cards with a photo of a naked woman on the back. Conner originally denied knowing anything about it but then, after his telephone call to me, admitted that it was his friend Jon's. He then proceeded to explain to Jane that he wasn't using it to masturbate. It was at that point that I walked in and Jane's jaw hit the floor. Conner immediately fled up the stairs.

Figuring it was likely well past time for the father/son talk, I slowly went up to his room. I sat down beside him and explained that the card was a problem because he had a younger sister and she and her friends might have found it. I explained that we did not want that to happen and he had to make sure that it didn't.

I also told him that we didn't really care if he was using the card to masturbate. I explained, very calmly, that if he wasn't masturbating now, he would be shortly and that it was natural and nothing to be ashamed of.

He looked at me with a sly little grin and said, "But Dad, what if I never masturbate?"

I kept a straight face as I told him, "Conner, if you never masturbate than you will be missing out on a really good time."

He collapsed in a fit of giggles and I quickly backed out the doorway and closed his door before he could see my face burning from embarrassment.

chapter nine

a closed door

I heard hushed voices downstairs and knew it was Kevin and Moira, all before I had truly woken up. I was still in that fugue-state, lost somewhere between sleep and wakefulness. Suddenly, I saw the profile of Conner's face right in front of me. It was as if he was leaning over me at that very moment. I reached my arms up to hold him but, of course, he wasn't there...at least not physically.

I then opened my eyes and my hands were in the air, reaching for him. As the fog of sleep withdrew, I knew that it was real, it was all real.

-Jane Luby

It was Sunday, another beautiful September day, and I was the first up. I had slept neither much nor well. I probably could have slept more but the dog had to go out. As was my habit, as soon as I walked out of our bedroom door, I looked down the hall to Conner's room. I was startled because the door was closed. If Conner's bedroom door was open, it meant that he was either away at school, out of town, or staying at a friend's house. If the bedroom door was closed, it meant that he was home, safe and sound.

That morning, looking down the hall and seeing the closed door, I was immediately reminded how much things had changed. As much as my head knew that he wasn't safe and asleep behind that closed door, my heart badly wanted him to be. I walked down the hall and opened the door. I looked around and gazed at the unmade bed and the clothes strewn around the floor. I sat down on the side of his bed and began to sob. I stayed as quiet as possible so as not to wake either Jane or Moira. Eventually, the dog nudged me and I went downstairs to let her out.

I then got on the computer downstairs to read the news reports about the accident and to look at Conner's Facebook page. The media reports were cold and clinical, with only flashing lights in the background behind the reporters. The outpouring of grief on his Facebook page was comforting but seemed, at least to me, detached from reality. Rationally, I understood that his friends' grief was genuine but it still didn't feel right. It didn't seem real. I understood that Conner was dead but emotionally I hadn't accepted it yet. It didn't feel like the door should be open. I was tempted to go back upstairs and close his door but I couldn't bring myself to do so. I wasn't yet ready to acknowledge that the door could never be shut again but I knew that I couldn't delude myself either.

Moira was the next up and we just sat in the kitchen, quietly talking and trying to figure out what the immediate future would be—what she might expect from the next couple of days. Neither of us was yet prepared to have an in-depth discussion about Conner and how our lives had just changed. Any discussion regarding our future lives could wait for another day. We focused on the here and now. We talked about the next few days and I let her know that she didn't need to return to school on Monday. She didn't have to return to school until she was ready to. She was scheduled to go on her Senior Retreat with her classmates from Jesuit High School the following weekend and, again, I let her know that the decision of whether or not to go was entirely up to her.

Jane got up shortly after that, and she looked awful. It was clear that she also had not slept either restfully or sufficiently. None of us had much of an appetite but we went through the motions of fixing at least something that resembled breakfast. We distracted ourselves from the grief by discussing who was coming into town and when. Jane's sister and her family were flying in from Canton. Her stepfather and his wife were flying in from South Bend. My mom and sisters were flying back from New England. My old friends, Tom Garrahan and Tony DiCioccio, were coming in sometime over the next couple of days.

We talked about the prayer vigil that would be held that night at Jesuit High School and that there would be a memorial mass there on Tuesday evening. We talked but avoided any mention of the accident. We weren't ready for that type of discussion yet.

The day flew by in a surreal haze. I found some relief in walking the dog through the park. It lent a semblance of normalcy to what was such an unnatural environment. It allowed me some "alone" time to escape the craziness and to embrace some solitude. I was, however, all too aware of the looks that I got from neighbors. We later came to refer to these as the "pity looks." They didn't have to say a word; we knew what these people were thinking... *Oh, those poor Lubys.* We came to hate the pity looks! They made us angry because we were never a family to be pitied. We were the ones to be envied. We were good-looking, successful, and—most importantly—happy. We had two great children, a dog and two cats. We lived in a nice house with the stereotypical white picket fence. We owned a Saab convertible and a Toyota minivan. We both had successful careers. We were the essence of suburban success. We were golden...until we weren't.

Sympathy was one thing. We could reluctantly accept sympathy. Empathy, while rare, was welcome. Pity, however, was entirely unwelcome, unacceptable, and completely resented.

At one point, I went to Costco to pick up some supplies for the visiting friends. I ran into a couple we'd played soccer with for a couple of years. I think that they might have seen me first but I was the first to walk up and say hello. Their discomfort was immediately noticeable and almost palpable. They didn't know what to say or how to say it. All they had to say was "We're sorry," but they couldn't do it. They mumbled something but it was clear that they wanted to get away from me as quickly as possible. I had become a pariah. Through no fault of my own, I was someone to avoid, someone unwelcome in others' lives. I was a reminder of what could happen to them and their children. I was the living embodiment of that fear in the back of every parent's mind.

Unfortunately, this was not to be the last time that people avoided us as a result of Conner's death. Jane and Moira experienced the same thing: the distancing of friends that resulted, ultimately and all too often, in the severing of friendships. We understood that being one of those "poor Lubys" made people uncomfortable. We didn't want that moniker any more than anyone else wanted to give it to us. Nonetheless, that is who we had become and some people just couldn't handle that.

The varying ways that friends and family dealt with Conner's death were truly shocking. We were pleasantly stunned by all of the support that we received. So many people came by the house just to let us know that they wanted to help, that they wanted to be there for us in whatever way we might need them. These were not just our friends but also Conner's and Moira's friends, and even some of their parents. There were stories and laughter to share, all of which made the days immediately following Conner's death so much easier. We weren't ready to say goodbye to Conner and hearing stories and talking about him helped make it feel as if he were still alive.

On the other hand, so many people that we considered good friends were absent, and their absence was obvious and disconcerting. Family friends our children had grown up with simply disappeared—no visit, no phone call, not even a sympathy card.

Over time, I have come to realize and accept that these lost friends and friendships were partly our fault. All in an instant, the three of us changed, and likely not for the better. We were more emotional. We could be scattered and have difficulty engaging in mindless banter. We could get angry at the slightest affront. It was sometimes a struggle to engage in the type of casual conversation that so many lightweight relationships are based upon. On one hand, we wanted to have these same lightweight conversations and relationships, but sometimes we just weren't up to the task.

Amongst the three of us, and with a small number of particularly close friends, we could revel in our very black and very warped sense of humor, which would, from time to time, devolve into abject impropriety. Ultimately, however, no matter how much we might laugh and seem to be coping, the grief was never far from the surface. Most people could sense our fragility. Some could be patient and help us weather the storm. For others, it was just too hard. They didn't like having to tread gingerly around our emotions. They couldn't handle the fact that our moods could change faster than the weather and that sometimes we would simply cry. We were not fun to be around when any of us were in the grips of grief. What do you say to someone who starts crying for no apparent reason other than the fact that his/her son or her brother just died?

For years, I thought about those who let us down, those who disappeared from our lives when we so desperately needed them. I tried to rationalize their actions. I blamed it on a lack of character. I blamed it on cowardice. I blamed it on an inherent deficiency of common decency. It was only over time and through one particular circumstance that I got a glimpse into how hard it must have been for all of our friends, both those that stayed around and those that didn't.

In September 2013, Trevor Sullivan died in a tragic motorcycle accident. Trevor's mother Pam had worked for me as a paralegal a few years before. Over the years, I got to know Pam, her husband and her children, including Trevor. They were a fun and raucous family. Trevor, in particular, was a gregarious and joyful young man, in many ways very similar to Conner.

When I received the phone call from a friend telling me of Trevor's death earlier that day, I immediately went over to Pam's home to offer my condolences. I knew what she and her husband were feeling. I understood the shock and grief that they were just starting to experience. I was going to be there for them—no pity looks, just sympathy and understanding. I would be a rock for them.

Despite all of this confidence and bravado, as I walked up their driveway, my stomach was in knots. I realized that I didn't know what to say to them or what to do. Over the previous several years I had written letters to parents who lost children. I knew how to express my condolences on paper and to write down my genuine sympathy. What I didn't know was how to look grieving parents in the eye and just talk to them, or more importantly how to shut up and just listen to them. I tried to think back to how I felt on that fateful Saturday and what I wanted people to say to me or do for me, but I realized that Pam and her family were much different than we were.

It quickly became clear that I had completely overestimated my ability to pave the way for them and to ease their pain. It was still too raw and fresh. They had only just learned of Trevor's death in Los Angeles. They were still processing the news and I was just another outsider, an unwelcome interloper.

My anger at those whom I believed had deserted us began to subside. For the first time in four years, I understood why we were pariahs to some people. I recognized that the discomfort those former friends felt wasn't necessarily a failure of character or any sort of cowardice. It was a natural feeling, one that I now fully and uncomfortably understood. I realized that I gave up on these friendships, not because of something they had done or not done, but because of my failure to understand them and what they were going through. Of course they could have, and they should have, done more, but at least now I understood why they didn't.

* * *

Moira had it tougher than either Jane or me. We had each other to rely upon. Certainly Moira had us but she also had to rely upon her friends and for a sixteen, and then seventeen, year old girl, many of her friends lacked the maturity to handle it. Moira's anger would flash more often. The fact that she kept so much inside resulted in periodic, but unpredictable, eruptions. She could have a very caustic tongue and was no longer interested in the teenage frivolity that her friends relished. She lacked patience for others. All of this drove many of Moira's friends away. They would be there one moment and gone the next. Their friendships became erratic and unpredictable, and Moira spent way too many Friday and Saturday nights of her senior year of high school at home with her parents. Her childhood had come to a complete and abrupt halt, and she had been thrust into a new reality—one that she was not, and could not at that age be, ready for. The death of her brother had become the principal turning point in her life. It marked the end of her childhood and the premature start to her life as an adult. Rather than a gradual transition, hers was immediate, jagged, and brittle.

Moira would now have to experience life not only as an only child but also as "the girl whose brother died." No longer would she have her brother to use as a measuring stick, to compare herself to, both positively and negatively. No longer would she have her brother to look out for her and to conspire with. No longer would she have her brother to console and encourage her. Unlike her peers, she would now have to live her life with the intimate knowledge of how fragile and how fleeting life can be.

Fortunately for all three of us, we forged an incredible bond. We were the only three who understood our loss, truly understood it, and we found great comfort in one another. We were the only three who could talk, openly and completely, about Conner. That is not to say that we never fought. Each of us could turn on the other on a dime. Fortunately, we came to understand why we did that and, over time, began to erupt less and less often. We learned to be patient with one another. We learned to turn the other cheek and to wait before responding. We learned to walk away when necessary.

The first true eruption that I remember happened about a week after the accident. The three of us had agreed that we didn't want to give any of Conner's belongings away yet and that all decisions regarding Conner and everything he left behind would be a joint decision, made by the three of us. Nonetheless, about a week after the accident, Jane stripped Conner's bed and washed the sheets.

Obviously, this was not an unusual process and, in normal times, we wouldn't have given it a second thought. Jane's motivation, of course, was that the sheets were dirty and that they needed to be washed. What she hadn't realized, however, was how often Moira and I, obviously at different times, had lain in those sheets just so that we could still smell Conner's scent. We often referred to Conner as the "Stinky Boy" because he was not always completely faithful to hygiene. He was too lazy to wash his sheets weekly and Jane generally had to nag him a bit to get it done. Accordingly, when he died, his sheets still carried his smell. It was oddly comforting to lie in his bed, close your eyes, and just smell. It made him seem closer. It made him seem less gone.

When we discovered that Jane had washed his sheets, Moira and I both blew up. It wasn't fair to Jane, and it certainly wasn't right, but our emotional fuses were short. The eruption thankfully didn't last too long and gradually faded into a pool of tears. Thereafter, we again agreed that decisions like that, no matter how ordinary or how simple, were to be discussed. This included our subsequent decision to box up his clothes and belongings, as well as our decision to give a portion of his ashes to friends to be spread around the world. More than ever before, we became a team; we became an incredibly tight-knit family—all because we had to. We were all we had left. We knew that we were the only ones we could rely upon—truly and completely rely upon.

chapter ten

i grieve

Cut to me waking up at 9:57 the morning of September 12th, my phone buzzing by my head with a call from his sister. It's the day after my roommate's 21st birthday. Talk about the worst hangover imaginable. And then make it worse. Conner is dead.

Despite me hoping beyond all hope, and thinking for more than a split second, that this was him being a douchebag and pulling some dumb prank, trying to prove to us all how much we really loved him...I mostly knew it was true. Dead. Gone. Forever.

And so the sun shines in L.A. and I'm on a plane within four hours back to Portland, trying not to cry next to a perfect stranger and not being able to think of anything other than that maybe—just maybe—Conner's soul would cross paths with mine at our 37,000 foot cruising altitude; me on my way home to a crushing homecoming; him on his way to....

-Megan McAninch

The call on that beautiful September morning became a sort of de-marcation, an incredibly short but sharp line that separates two entirely different, yet achingly similar, lives. Prior to The Call, I had led what many would consider to be a charmed life. I don't want to suggest that I *didn't* have a charmed life, for I surely did. It wasn't, perhaps, quite as charmed as many people thought. There are three reasons for this misperception. First of all, I had a tendency to share my successes publicly but to keep my failures private. Secondly, as I am generally an upbeat person, many people assume that my happiness is born of success. Finally, I have long had a tendency to live beyond my means, which gave me the appearance of being more financially successful than I actually was.

In most aspects, my life *was* charmed and one that was likely far better than I deserved. I had a wonderful marriage and two great children; my business was successful; everyone was healthy; and my worries were minimal. The problems, however, were there. Debt was always a specter following me around and causing innumerable squabbles with Jane about spending. The kids' academics were always a point of contention such that my attempts to assist with homework often resulted in tears. I don't want to minimize the work or worry that was involved in that life but, at least in hindsight, these problems were relatively minor and, also in hindsight, completely and utterly trivial. It was my golden age.

After The Call, life was much different. The charm was gone. As a family, Conner's death was the first of many subsequent downturns and events that affected all of us. The Call seemed to open the floodgates of misfortune. The recession, the temporary failure of my business, the loss of the office building that we'd invested our life savings in, the loss of our home to foreclosure, the illness and death of our beloved dog, my mother's death, my diagnosis of leukemia—The Call seemed to initiate a lengthy and painful slide that lasted well over three years. None of that seemed possible before The Call, but it all became too real afterward. We were always waiting for the next shoe to drop and it usually did. It was no longer a matter of *if* something bad would happen but, rather, *when* it would happen and what it would be? A lifetime of good fortune was being evened out, all within an incredibly and painfully short span of time.

It all started with Conner's death. The loss of a child is, perhaps, every parent's greatest fear. It is a fear that is rarely shared with anyone, not even with a spouse, but is always present in the back of one's mind. It may come to the fore if a child suffers a serious injury or illness but otherwise is rarely spoken of. Most times it is just a slight, but perni-cious, tingling of danger deep in the shadows of our minds. As parents, you avoid thinking about it or talking about it, but the fear always lurks in the shadows and only comes to the light in the darkest of moods.

When your child dies, the loss creates a feeling of emptiness in your psyche, making us feel less than whole. A friend of mine explained this by comparing it to the feeling of losing a parent. She explained that when you lose a parent, you have lost someone you are a part of. When you lose a child, you are losing someone who is a part of you. Perhaps it is a distinction without a difference but I understood the explanation.

As I grew older, I, like most adult children, grew apart from my parents. While I loved them and remained a part of them and their lives, they became a smaller part of mine. When they died, I was saddened and certainly mourned their deaths, but *my* family was the overwhelm-ing focus of my life. The deaths of my parents became little more than an acknowledgment of the changing of the seasons and the passing of the years. Even with my parents gone, I still had my family and my life. With Conner's death, I no longer had either.

* * *

Sometimes the emptiness caused by Conner's death is close to the sur-face and other times it is buried deep within. The emptiness could feel like a dull ache or, alternatively, a searing pain that was all-consuming. It created a weariness that was both emotional and physical. It became tempting to give in to the weariness, to just block out the world and retreat into the darkness.

The weariness, in turn, created a form of numbness that actually provided an odd but welcome measure of comfort and relief. The wea-riness and numbness allowed me to retreat from reality. It allowed me to pretend that everything was all right again, that everything was normal. It allowed me to imagine that the sun might shine again, that I might laugh again…someday.

The degree to which a parent gives in to this temptation to "go dark," and the depth of such darkness, is largely dependent upon the parent's emotional health, as well as the support received from friends and family. Every mourning parent, at least to a certain extent and for at least some period of time, gives into this temptation to go dark. For most, it is a temporary respite from the world and the pain of the loss; for some it is more permanent and crippling. For me, it was and is a bit of both.

* * *

Grief is, of course, a completely subjective and inevitable emotion. It is subjective in that there are no set parameters and no measurables. Most people are familiar with the five stages of grief, a model first proposed by Elisabeth Kübler-Ross. Those stages are denial, anger, bargaining, depression, and acceptance. The difficulty with this model is that it is generally interpreted in much too simplistic a fashion. Not all people experience each stage. I know that I never experienced either denial or bargaining. As soon as I heard the news of the accident, I knew that there was no question that Conner was dead. In my mind, there was no way to deny that fact and no one with whom to bargain. This was not a case of mistaken identification. My son was dead.

Also, the Kübler-Ross stages are not linear. The stages reappear and repeat themselves, sometimes overlapping and sometimes spaced far apart. Even after acceptance—and I question what that term really means—there is still depression and anger is never far away. The fact that I was able to accept Conner's death didn't end my grieving. In fact, I came to the acceptance stage pretty quickly. I knew he would not be coming home again. I knew that I would never hear his voice again. I knew that I would never be able to give him a hug and a kiss. I accepted the fact that I would never be able to see the man he would have become. The depression stage, at least for me, was the most frequent recurring stage—and it keeps recurring, perhaps in some way, because

I welcome it. Through the depression, I am able to keep Conner alive because I know I won't forget him that way. The fear of forgetting him has replaced my earlier fear of losing him.

Over the years following Conner's death, we have created new memories—of holidays and vacations, hiking and rafting, concerts and plays. In none of those memories is Conner present. Graduations, birthdays, and anniversaries come and go, all without him. We talk about him during these events, but he is never there other than in our thoughts and in our hearts. When we discuss memories of particular events, it becomes an increasing struggle to remember whether Conner was a part of the particular event or if it happened after his death.

As these new memories are created, they tend to blot out some of the older ones. I began to forget some of my funny stories with, and about, Conner. I began to forget what his voice sounded like. I have difficulty seeing his face when I close my eyes. I look at his friends and compare their maturing faces and Conner's forever-youthful face in the numerous photographs around the house and office. Each time I realize that my memory of him is fading with time, I experience guilt anew and the pain returns. What kind of father forgets what his child sounds like or looks like? What kind of monster can create new and wonderful memories, none of which involve his only son? This ever-renewing sense of grief and shame became the cilice and hairshirt that I punished myself with. The pain became my penance for the sin of letting his memory fade. The sin of failing as a father.

* * *

For me, the grief in the weeks after the accident was palpable. I walked around as a functioning zombie. I couldn't give in to the grief because I had my obligations—to my wife and daughter, to our friends and family, and to all who needed me to show them how to deal with this loss. A friend at the gym complimented me for making it easier for others to be around me in the weeks and months following Conner's death. He saw my stoicism as something to be proud of rather than recognizing it as the cowardice it really was. My apparent stoicism was nothing more than a mask that I hid behind.

Of all of my obligations, perhaps the most important was to myself. I couldn't, and wouldn't, allow myself to give in to the grief, other than for brief moments and never within the view of others. I was afraid that if I did give in and dove into that vast pool, I might never come out. I was torn. One part of me wanted to let the grief envelop me and provide me with a measure of relief. I'm not sure what relief there would actually be other than the relief of letting go and giving in to all of the emotion. The rational part of me understood, however, that I couldn't do that. I needed to be strong. I needed to keep myself together emotionally, at least to the extent that others could observe. I needed to wear that mask of strength so as to be able to provide support to my family and friends. To do otherwise would have been to disgrace the memory of Conner. To do otherwise would have been to let my family down. To do otherwise would have shown my true weakness.

Accordingly, within days after the accident, I went back to the office. I would try to work and maintain at least a semblance of normalcy. In reality, I might get an hour or so of work in but then, behind the closed door of my office, I would simply stare at pictures of Conner and our family or read the online articles about the accident and the sometimes-cruel comments people posted on media websites. I used my office as an excuse to hide from family and friends.

I went to the gym and tried to work out. I found, however, that it was more difficult than I imagined. Any exercise that allowed my mind to roam became unbearable as my thoughts always led me back to Conner and the details of the accident. More and more, my imagination began to picture what the crash had really been like. I would imagine myself in Conner's place or, alternatively, off to the side watching the car crash and burn. In spite of myself, my mind always went there. When it got to be too much for me, I would find quiet places at the gym to hide and be alone. I would sit against a wall, to all appearances just catching my breath, but in reality fighting back the tears.

My experience in maintaining a façade of success helped me maintain a similar façade of normalcy. While I became adept at fooling others in how I dealt with my grief, I could not fool myself. The cracks in my psyche were pronounced and they showed in different ways. Sometimes I masked my grief with misguided attempts at humor. Other times, my anger would erupt at unexpected times and for unwarranted reasons. Fortunately, I don't have a natural affinity for drugs or alcohol, although I attempted to find relief through both. As soon as I realized that neither provided any real comfort, I discarded that route.

The grief also had an effect on my marriage. It created a strain that remained for years after the accident. The strain most commonly came to the fore due to our sometimes-fumbling attempts to console one another. I knew (or at least believed) that I was emotionally stronger than Jane. I knew that I had to comfort her when she was overwhelmed with grief. I learned to hold her and just let her cry into my shoulder. I learned when to offer words of comfort and when to hold her without saying a word.

As a result of keeping my grief private, it usually went without comfort or ease. Jane always tried to console me when the emotions came to be too much for me. The problem was that when she tried to console, she would succumb to the grief and join me in despair. I could feel her breaking. At that point, I had to put my own grief aside, slip the mask back on and console her. I found no comfort or solace in my wife's tears. It was frustrating that she could not provide me with the comfort that I needed but was unable to accept. At these times, I resented her both for her ability to openly grieve and for her inability to find a way to provide me with solace.

The truth was that only one person could have comforted me and he was now dead—the focus of my grief.

* * *

I learned to hide my grief and to keep the mask firmly in place. I only allowed it to surface when I was alone. Sometimes this would involve a solitary drive in the car, and other times I would go to Conner's bench.

We had a bench installed in Cook Park, not far from our home. The bench overlooks a small boat dock on the Tualatin River where Conner used to fish for crawdads when he was much younger. The location of the bench is busy in the summer and very peaceful in the fall and winter. The plaque on the bench reads:

CONNER PATRICK LUBY
10/25/88 – 9/12/09
MAC DEARTHÁIR CARA

The inscription says, in Gaelic, "Son Brother Friend." Nothing could describe Conner better than that.

At the dedication of the bench on the one-year anniversary of the accident, we had a large group of friends there to celebrate. One person attending was an attorney friend of mine. Jack Lundeen and I were friends, albeit on a more professional than personal basis, but I certainly appreciated the fact that he was there.

At one point, he and I were talking and I mentioned how "the boy" would have loved the bench. Jack interrupted me and said, "You mean your son." I said, "Yeah, the boy." He repeated, "You mean your son." It then hit me that Jack thought I was starting to disassociate and distance myself from Conner in a subconscious effort to protect myself from the grief. I chuckled and then explained to him that "the boy" was just one of Conner's nicknames. When talking *to* Conner, I almost always called him "Moo" or "MooMoo" or one of a few other select nicknames. When talking about him, I always referred to him as "the boy," in the same way that I always referred to Moira as "the girl."

I found the bench to be of immense comfort. One fall evening, I went there to just spend time with Conner. A wedding was going on nearby. I found the gaiety to be both comforting and saddening. It was nice to hear laughter and joy and know that a couple was beginning a new journey, surrounded by friends and families. It reminded me, however, of the fact that Conner would never celebrate his wedding with a bride and their friends. I sat at the bench, closed my eyes, and let my conflicting emotions float slowly out over the river.

Other times, I just go to the bench and enjoy the solitude. I might lie down on it as the low murmur of the river lulls me into a state of serenity. At those times, I can take the mask off, let my mind wander, and consider what should have been. I can gaze up at the stars and wonder if his spirit is still somewhere out there. I can dream of once again speaking with him and asking him what happened, of asking him what the hell he had been thinking when he climbed into the Saab that evening for the drive home. I can dream of, once again, giving him a hug and a kiss and telling him, just one more time, that I love him and hearing those words from him.

The bench has become the place where, rain or shine, I can grieve, completely and unabashedly. I can experience my grief in a way that I never could anywhere else, not even with Jane. I hope that one day I may be able to share my grief with her but I doubt that that day will ever come. I'm not sure that I am strong enough for that.

* * *

Whether private or public, grief, over time, becomes more sporadic and, eventually, less powerful. That is just the nature of the beast. It's not that time heals all wounds, for there could be no true healing of a wound such as this. Time does, however, seem to lessen the pain of the wound and we adapt without ever truly or fully healing.

At first the grief was constantly present and always threatening to overwhelm me. Eventually, however, I began to see grief like ocean waves. Sometimes I would see a wave of grief approaching in the distance and could gird myself for it. This might happen on the anniversary of Conner's death, his birthday, or the holidays. The actual day being celebrated was usually bearable because I was prepared for it. Often, we would be surrounded by friends and family and, as a result, by stories and laughter. Afterward, however, when the friends and family members went back to their lives, all bets were off and the grief would punish me. When the dark fell, when the quiet came, when there was solitude—*that* was when the wave would break. That was when I would give myself permission to break, but always and only when I was completely alone.

There were also sneaker waves of grief. For anyone who doesn't live near a coast, sneaker waves are waves that don't appear large or dangerous from a distance but that sneak up and surprise you. Every year, sneaker waves drag people out to sea to drown. Grief became like that. I might be at work or out with friends or just mowing the lawn when, all of a sudden, tears were pouring down my face. Without warning or relief, the reality and finality of Conner's death would press itself upon me. The understanding that Conner was gone, really and eternally gone, would hit me. All of a sudden, the scab would be ripped off again and the pain would be as strong and raw as on that first day.

At Conner's memorial mass, three days after his death, a woman I didn't recognize approached me. She offered me her condolences and then said, "I lost my son a few years ago."

I pulled back and looked at her. She was dry-eyed but I could still see the pain in her eyes without knowing whether it was pain for her son or for Conner. I asked her, quite simply, "When does the pain go away?"

She shook her head. "Never," she said. "It never goes away. It changes but it never goes away."

I thanked her and she walked away. I never saw her again but still think of her often.

chapter eleven
charm

I was the faculty administrator at the boys' soccer game. It was my job to make sure that the students maintained the appropriate level of support. At one point in the first half, I heard someone yell, "Ref...you suck!" I looked and it was, of course, Conner.

I walked over to him and explained to him that that type of language was not acceptable from a Jesuit student. I explained that if he took umbrage at a bad call by the referee, he would need to find a more appropriate way to express his displeasure.

It was in the second half when the referee again made a questionable call and this time I heard from the Jesuit stands, "Ref...I take umbrage at the call!" All I could do was look at Conner and laugh.

-Christopher Smart
Dean of Students
Jesuit High School

Conner always used his charm on his teachers. Throughout grade school and middle school, it was not unusual for us to see a report card with grades that were mediocre, or worse, but the teacher would say that he was a pleasure to have in class. We knew that he needed more structure and decided to try and get him into Jesuit High School. Jesuit High School was, and is, the premier Catholic high school in the area. While the local public high school, Tigard High, was a relatively good school, it suffered from overcrowding and we knew Conner wouldn't get the type of attention that he needed in order to succeed academically.

We explained all of this to him but he, of course, wanted to stay with his friends and go to Tigard High. We made a deal with him. We told him that if he would complete the application process, and use his best efforts, we would then have a family discussion before determining where he would end up going, assuming that he was accepted by Jesuit High School. This seemed to appease his worries and we proceeded with the application.

Another reason that I wanted him to attend Jesuit High School was that, in middle school, he had started to exhibit an anti-religious bias. I certainly have those biases myself but they come from a lifetime of exposure to religion and my exploration and study of the various mythologies that comprise Western religions. I was unwilling to have Conner just assume an anti-religious bias without working for it. I wanted him to be exposed to Christianity by those with true faith, both teachers and fellow students. If he chose to believe in Christianity or another religion, I was fine with that, as long as he made the knowing decision to believe or not.

We were very fortunate in that Conner benefited from this type of exposure. While he never became truly religious, he did become both spiritual and accepting of others' faiths.

Now I should explain that I'm pretty good at knowing how to play the game when I have to. I knew that having gone to Regis College in Denver, a Jesuit institution, would help with Conner's application. I knew that having graduated from Notre Dame Law School would help. I also knew that most of the kids at Jesuit High School came from the various local Catholic grade schools rather than public schools like Conner did. Accordingly, I volunteered and became a Minister of Welcome at St. Anthony's Catholic Church in Tigard. These ministers are the people who help seat people for the masses and collect the donations. That's it.

We weren't regular churchgoers and I would have described myself at the time as being agnostic, but I was willing to play the part of devout Catholic for the chance to get my son into Jesuit High School. This required me to keep my mouth shut more than I was comfortable in doing; but being a parent, you do what you have to do.

Part of the admissions process for Jesuit High School is a personal interview. Each prospective student and their parents interview with a representative from the school. On the day set for our interview, we met with a nice older lady in the school's library. Given Conner's grades, we didn't hold out much hope that we would be successful, and this allowed us to be very relaxed in the interview process. We were laughing and joking and Conner was as charming as ever. I really think that the interviewer liked our family and the fact that we seemed to enjoy and truly love one another. I think she saw that we were the type of people that would be welcome additions to the Jesuit High School community. What we didn't know at the time, and for this I will always be grateful, is that our interviewer was Sandy Satterburg, the school's principal.

A month or so later, we got the letter of acceptance. Jane and I were ecstatic. We called Conner downstairs and congratulated him on being accepted into Jesuit High School. We told him that we were certain he was going to love it and excel there. He looked somewhat askance and said, "But you told me that if I made a good faith effort that we would talk about whether I was going to Jesuit or if I could go to Tigard."

I looked at him with a big smile and said, "Conner, we *did* just talk about it…and you're going to Jesuit. Congratulation!"

He failed to see the humor in my response but understood that I had, at least technically, been true to my word so the grousing was relatively minimal. In fact, I think deep down, he liked the idea of going to Jesuit High School. He knew that it was a prestigious school and that it was quite the accomplishment to be accepted, something that many of his friends from middle school couldn't have achieved. While it took him a few months to settle in, by the time that Christmas of his freshman year rolled around, he was Jesuit through and through.

Conner made his mark on Jesuit High School, certainly as much as it made his mark on him. On his very first day of school, he was put on academic probation. We were called into the Dean of Academics' office and this was the first, but certainly not the last, time we met with Paul Hogan. While Paul eventually became a friend, his role as Dean of Academics meant that he had to be the hard-ass on academic issues. He sternly explained to us that Conner had gotten a final grade of D in Algebra in his last semester of eighth grade. He told us that had he known of that before the letters of acceptance had gone out, Conner would not be attending Jesuit High School.

As we walked out of the Dean's office, we looked sternly at Conner. He replied with a sly smile and a shrug. He certainly wasn't proud of his grades but neither was he embarrassed. Grades just were not that important to him.

What *was* important was making an impression on people. He impressed the gym teacher by setting a freshman record for pull-ups. His years of rock climbing had given him great upper body strength. This then led him to join the track team and take up pole vaulting. He cleared ten feet his freshman year and earned a varsity letter.

Other than pole vaulting that freshman year, Conner did not have much interest in participating in sports. This was not from a lack of interest or ability but, rather, from a lack of drive. He found greater enjoyment from watching others experience success than by putting the work in himself. While I understand why others might consider this a character flaw, I don't. It was just his nature to find joy in the successes and accomplishments of others rather than in his own.

We knew that he had been a big supporter of the cheerleading squad but, after his death, we found out that he also used to bring snacks to the soccer teams, both the boys' and girls' teams. He was one of the ringleaders at basketball games who came up with creative cheers, as well as questionable jibes at opposing teams and their fans. One season, Conner and the other students brought umbrellas to the basketball games, and every time a Jesuit player hit a three-point shot, they would open the umbrellas and yell, "IT'S RAINING THREES!!!"

* * *

As Jesuit High School had a relatively strict dress code, Conner learned to express his individuality with his hair. He experimented with different styles and different colors. In his junior year, his amateurish attempt to color his hair resulted in his hair turning from dirty blond to gray. With absolutely no embarrassment but, rather, a measure of pride, he "rocked" his gray hair for the better part of a month. He subsequently dyed his hair from blond to black and many different colors in-between. He wore it long or medium-length.

No hairstyle was off-limits. One time he came back from a retreat with his hair braided into cornrows. He was certainly as vain as any other high school student, but he enjoyed shocking people with the style and/or color of his hair or his outrageous comments.

He developed friendships with everyone, refusing to settle into any particular clique. He became friends with the jocks and the eggheads, as well as the musicians and actors. His friendships crossed all religious, racial, and political boundaries. They had no limits. If he found someone to be interesting, he sought out his or her friendship and he was always there for his friends.

At one point in his senior year, I was retained to evict some tenants from a residence in Beaverton. It turned out that the tenants were the family of one of Conner's classmates. I had met the classmate, Jude, on a number of occasions and he was a very polite young man. He had even slept at our house a time or two. I told Conner about the eviction because I recognized that it could be an uncomfortable situation for him. I tried negotiating a resolution but was unsuccessful and ultimately obtained a judgment from the court to evict them. I arranged for the sheriff to change the locks on the doors to the residence and was preparing to have the family's belongings seized by the police.

The night we had the locks changed, it was Back-To-School Night at Jesuit High School. Jane and I were meeting with Conner's teachers when I received a call from Conner. "Dad, guess where I am?" Conner asked.

"I don't know, Monkey Boy," I said. "Where are you?"

"I'm at Jude's house," he told me blithely.

I paused for a moment, uncertain as to what he was doing and why, and then said, "Conner, how did you get in there? We changed the locks."

"We broke in through a window," he told me. "Don't worry, we didn't damage it. I'm helping Jude and his family move their stuff out."

I smiled. "Here's the deal, Moo," I told him. "Make sure that they get everything out tonight because if they are there tomorrow, they, *and you*, will probably get arrested for trespass. Understand?"

"Understood," he told me, still casual. "By the way, Dad, can Jude stay with us for a couple of days until his mom finds a new place for them to live?"

I chuckled quietly and told him, as he knew I would, "Of course."

I was so proud of my boy. He was not only willing to help a friend, but he was unabashed about breaking into a locked home to do so because it was the right thing to do.

* * *

When his sister started at Jesuit High School, Conner was both proud and envious. He was proud of the lovely young woman that his sister was becoming, but he was also a bit envious of her confidence. While Conner always exuded a certain bravado in public, he really suffered from a genuine, but wholly unwarranted, lack of self-confidence. It was this sense of self-confidence that he always envied in his little sister.

Despite the fact that Conner warned his friends to leave his little sister alone, it became a challenge to see which of his classmates could "nail" his little sister. Fortunately, Moira was smart and tough enough not to fall for any of that foolishness. I remember explaining to her that any senior who hit on a freshman, a girl three or more years younger, had problems. I asked her what she would think if any of her freshman classmates started dating a sixth grader. She responded that it would be creepy. I then pointed out that the age difference was exactly the same. That may have been when she started mocking any of Conner's friends who tried to hit on her.

Many of Conner's closest friends took Moira under their wings. She became a cheerleader and many of the older girls, already friends of Conner's, became big sisters to her— something that would become particularly important in the coming years. A number of Conner's guy friends also became protective older brothers. While having a sister at the same school may have cramped his style a bit, there was never a doubt that he was incredibly proud of her.

* * *

I have never been a big fan of tattoos. When Conner was young, I frequently pointed out people who tried to distinguish themselves by dressing outrageously or with tattoos and piercings. I would explain to him that this was simply a sad attempt by these people to call attention to themselves. I felt that it was truly unfortunate if they believed that tattoos were the best way that they could make their mark in this world. I always believed that it was better to have people notice you for who you are, and for what you have done, rather than just for how you look. I neither understood nor recognized that, for many, this was a way to make a statement of nonconformity and individuality.

I remember having a conversation with one of Conner's high school classmates when he was showing off a new tattoo. I asked him why he did it and he proclaimed that he was expressing his individuality. I then commented on the fact that many people seemed to be getting tattoos, and he commented that it was, in fact, very popular to get inked. He failed to see the irony in that and I didn't bother to point it out to him.

Despite my repeated reminders, and perhaps because of his affinity for shocking others, Conner got his first tattoo on his eighteenth birthday. The tattoo was of four stars, of gradually increasing size, on the right side of his chest. They were just five-pointed stars without any coloration and not filled-in. He proudly showed them to us on the day after his birthday, and we quickly dubbed them his "stripper stars."

I like to think that he chose the number of stars to represent the number of people in our family but I don't really know. I do know that he was more proud of having gotten the tattoos than he was *of* the tattoos. It was as if he was proud of having made the decision, even if he wasn't entirely proud of the decision itself. He had made an adult decision and that was enough for him.

A year or so later, some friends talked him into getting a tattoo on the inside of his bottom lip. The tattoo read, "I Kick Ass!" We didn't learn about that tattoo for over six months. Eventually, Moira "narc'd" on him. When Jane next saw Conner, she called him over and said that she wanted to check his teeth to see if they had moved at all after his braces were taken off. As she pulled down his lip, she expressed mock surprise to find the tattoo. I'm not sure that Conner ever found out that Jane knew about the tattoo before "finding" it.

On the Monday after the accident, I took Moira, one of her friends and four of Conner's friends down to a local tattoo parlor to get the same lip tattoo. Subsequently, another twenty-five or so of Conner's friends got that lip tattoo. Jane and I finally got ours on the second anniversary of Conner's death.

And yes, it was incredibly painful.

* * *

One of the great things about Jesuit High School is that college is not just an option for the students but, rather, it is expected. Every single member of Conner's graduating class went on to college. For Conner, there was only one college that was acceptable – Arizona State University. He and I took a trip to Arizona during his senior year and visited the University of Arizona and Northern Arizona University, in addition to ASU. While he may have checked out these other schools, there was never any doubt. It was ASU and only ASU.

Arizona State University had a well-earned reputation as a party school and it was a flame to Conner's moth. The heat and the girls were an irresistible attraction and, when he was accepted there, it was understood by all of us that ASU was where his future would lie.

We all flew down to Arizona in August 2007 to drop Conner off at school. Even before he arrived in Tempe, Conner had friends there. Through social media, he had met a number of incoming freshmen and started the social aspect of college life well before ever setting foot on campus. As soon as we got there and located his dorm, he informed us that he needed to help a couple of freshman girls he knew move into their rooms. He hadn't met them in person yet, but they were cute and needed a hand.

After finally getting him set up in his dormitory room and meeting his new roommate, we walked down to Mill Street, which is the main street just off campus. As we were walking down the street, we heard someone yell, "Conner!" Conner turned around and, almost immediately, greeted Aaron by name. This was one of his new classmates, this one from New Jersey, that Conner had met online.

* * *

ASU was both a blessing and a curse for Conner. He understood that he had to attend classes, but there were parties every night and beautiful girls everywhere. In October, he sent me a photograph. He was lying out by one of the pools between two young ladies. They were topless and he had his arms outstretched, covering their breasts. The look on his face could only be described as being a "shit-eating grin."

While making all sorts of new friends at ASU, he managed to maintain many of his older friendships. Friends like Larry Floyd would drive to Tempe for a weekend visit and Conner took a twelve-hour bus trip to Los Angeles just to spend some time with Megan McAninch on her nineteenth birthday. Distance was never a deterrent for him when he felt the need to spend time with a friend.

In addition to friends, new and old, Conner maintained his love for his family. We talked almost every day and he would regale us with stories—some sordid, some just plain funny. In the winter of 2007-08, his sister was participating in the State Championships for Cheerleading. At Conner's urgent request, we flew him home for the weekend without telling Moira.

Now the cheerleading squad takes their competitions very seriously and has certain traditions. In the days before the State Championship, they always have a team dinner and then gather at the Jesuit High School Chapel to meet with family and friends. The cheerleaders sit and listen to people tell them how happy and proud they are of each of them. It is always very emotional and absolutely wonderful for everyone there—cheerleaders, classmates, friends and family alike.

As Moira was just a sophomore, we let some of the parents of the older kids speak first. Eventually, I got up and told Moira that we had a special gift for her. At that point, Conner walked in the back door. Immediately, she ran to him, tears of joy running down her face. Conner told everyone how much he loved his little sister and how proud he was of her.

Our hope is that the words spoken that evening stay with Moira forever.

* * *

At the conclusion of his freshman year at ASU, Conner came home for the summer. His grades, while passing, were not good enough to warrant us continuing to pay out-of-state tuition. We strongly encouraged him to attend a local community college until he could improve his grades. He reluctantly agreed but never gave up his dream of returning to ASU. The friendships that he had developed there were too deep to consider graduating anywhere else.

Unfortunately, this may have been one of our bigger mistakes. While Conner attended local community college, he regressed. He fell into the same rut that many of his friends had fallen into. This was a rut resulting from a combination of a lack of direction and ambition. Community college brought him no joy and, without any sense of direction, he lacked the ambition to learn just for the sake of learning. At least at ASU, his friends were moving toward graduation. With the transfer to community college, he lost his way.

He began working at various hookah bars around town and found a wonderful outlet for extending his network of friends. It might help to explain the culture of hookah. Obviously, it has roots in the Middle East and, with a significant Arab population in the Portland area, there were a number of hookah bars. They didn't serve alcohol so you only needed to be eighteen years old to go there. Hookah bars were very popular at the time because they allowed young people, too old for high school activities but too young for bars, a place to get together.

Jane and I would, on occasion, come into whichever hookah bar Conner was working at the time. He would always get the biggest of smiles and promptly introduce his "Mom and Dad" to everyone. He was never ashamed to have his folks show up. He never felt like it wasn't cool to have his parents there.

While Conner loved spending time with his friends, he gradually began to understand the depth and breadth of the rut he was in. He eventually stopped attending community college and was having difficulty envisioning his future. This was the spring of 2009. I could sense how much this was bothering him. He felt as if he was disappointing us and, if truth be told, he was.

We knew, apparently more than he did, what he was capable of. We had much more confidence in him than he had in himself. The rut became a source of tension between us and created a burden upon him that threatened to destroy everything that was so wonderful about him. He began putting on weight and sleeping more, all the symptoms of the beginning stages of depression. He became moody and his anger flared at trivial affronts. The boy of unlimited potential seemed to be lost.

The problem was that none of us really knew how to help him. Being his father, I always knew what he *should* do but I also knew that he had to figure his own way out—by himself and his way. I could only watch and wait, hoping that he would find the solution sooner rather than later. I could only make recommendations, and I did; but they could only be recommendations and, even then, they generally fell on deaf ears. I made sure that he knew that I would always be there when he needed me, but he was at that point in his life where he didn't want to need me anymore.

Conner had to find out on his own what he wanted to do with his life. Fortunately for all of us, toward the end of the summer of 2009, he finally did.

chapter twelve
the club

My Dad died my senior year of high school in a sudden accident. I came back to school shortly after it happened, still in complete shock. One of the toughest things about my return was the fact that no one would talk to me about it. Everyone knew what had happened, and I knew they knew. Most people were either too scared or felt too awkward to know what to say, so they remained silent or made small talk. That was so painful because I wanted to talk about my Dad and his death. I needed to talk about what had happened but had neither the place nor the opportunity to do so.

I was in a stupor when I walked into Mr. Carver's religion class. I always sat next to Conner and did so again that day. The first thing he said when I sat down was, "Oh my God, what happened?"

That was exactly what I needed—someone to talk to me about the only thing I could think about, someone to let me know they cared, someone to be there for me when I needed it. I needed that blunt question and it couldn't have come from a better person. He wasn't making a show of asking, he wasn't asking to be nosy, but he was asking because he cared. Of all the interactions after the most difficult event of my life, his still sticks out in my mind after seven years. This may have seemed small to him or to most people, but Conner had a gift of being honest, open, and saying what he was thinking, and that can be exactly what people need a lot of the time. No small talk, no beating around the bush, just honesty and openness from one person to another.

-Andrea Schluderman

It was only a couple of months after the accident and I was still trying to come to terms with this new life of mine. Life certainly felt familiar and had many of the same attributes but yet was so different. I still worked; I still exercised; I still ate and slept and did the other things that I do in the normal course of my life. Now, however, I did them under the shadow of Conner's death.

One day I was at the gym and trying to work out. While before I was very social and talked to the people that I customarily saw there, now I tended to avoid those people. I was more solitary and quiet. I still wanted to exercise but, no matter how hard I tried, I couldn't get things back to the way they had been. I didn't want to make small talk. I didn't want to hear others' problems. I just wanted to clear my head and replace the emotional pain with the ache of sore muscles.

As I was sitting on a bench taking a break from weightlifting, Quinton Hess came over and sat down beside me. Quinton was one of the familiar faces that I would nod to from time to time but I had never really spoken with him. He looked at me and said, "Welcome to the Club."

I must have had a quizzical look on my face as he looked from my face down to the floor and simply said, "I lost my son seven years ago."

There it was. There was the opening that allowed me to start talking. While I could speak in objective terms with friends and family, Quinton became the first person I could really talk to about what I was going through. He was the first person who could tell me, as a father, what to expect in the coming months.

He explained that his son had been cleaning his shotgun when it accidently went off. Like Conner, it made no sense. It was one of those ridiculous and senseless mistakes that have such tragic and lasting consequences.

I had created my first new bond since Conner died. Quinton explained to me that the "Club" was one that no one ever wanted to join but that had a surprisingly large membership. He explained that there were members everywhere and in plain sight, you just needed to spot them. I was not the first person to have lost a child and certainly wouldn't be the last.

As I came to understand the number of people who were part of the Club I hadn't known about, I marveled at their strength and empathy. Others would come up to me at the gym or in the store and share their stories with me. Being able to share this common bond with others seemed to provide a measure of relief from the grief.

Over the coming years, I decided to "pay forward" the kindness that Quinton and the others had extended to me. Thereafter, whenever I heard about a child in the area that died, I reached out to the parents. Rather than approaching them directly and, perhaps, being seen as an unwelcome interloper, I would write them a letter. The letter merely let them know that they were not alone; that there were others that completely understood the depth and breadth of the grief that they were feeling. I let them know that Jane and I would always be available if they ever needed to talk. I explained that it was sometimes easier to talk to a stranger than to friends, especially if they needed to talk about the dark and stormy depths of their grief. I promised to never subject them to the "pity look."

Most recipients responded with a simple thank you and never followed up on my offers to talk. Nonetheless, I hope that my letters did some good.

I think that Conner would be proud of me for doing this.

* * *

After being welcomed to the Club, I began to wonder about how other parents deal with similar, but different, situations. I've known friends who have lost children to drug addiction. They're just waiting for the phone call that tells them that their son or daughter overdosed and died. I've seen friends whose children have rejected them and removed themselves from their parents' lives. I've seen marriages dissolve in acrimony and bitterness. I've seen people suffering from debilitating diseases.

I've seen people who were giving up because life just became too overwhelming.

Is there any sort of community for them? Who reaches out to them?

I began to reflect on the nature of grief in general and how broad an emotion it can be. Certainly, all of these people have reason to grieve. Was my grief any greater than what these people experience? In looking back over the years, I realize that my grief was likely less than others'. My grief is, and was, tempered by the fact that I have so many wonderful memories of Conner. I know that I had a great relationship with Conner, at least most of the time, and most importantly, at the time of his death. I know that on the day he died, he truly and completely loved me and he knew that I truly and completely loved him. On the day he died, I know that he was just as proud of being my son as I was of being his father. While I know that I'll never see him again in this life, I have a lifetime of memories to cherish. Further, I still have my wife and daughter and they bring me immeasurable amounts of pride and joy.

While my grief may be less than others, it is no less real and I wouldn't want it any other way. Whether great or small, I find that I don't want the pain to go completely away. The pain reminds me of my love for Conner. Again, you cannot grieve if you have not loved, and I need to be reminded of how much I loved, and still love, Conner and how much I have lost. The pain is my reminder. This becomes even more important as the years go by. Conner was far too important, and far too wonderful a son and human being, to be forgotten.

* * *

Shortly before Moira's twenty-first birthday, she and I were talking and she made a statement that startled me. She told me that she couldn't imagine what it was like to have a brother. At that point, it had been slightly more than five years since his death. Certainly she remembered Conner and had many wonderful memories of him and our family from before his death. What she was saying, however, was that her void was starting to be filled with new memories and experiences. She still missed him and still mourned his death but she was becoming whole again. These new experiences and memories were crowding out the grief.

She found that she missed talking to him less and less often. She found other ears and shoulders to rely on when she needed to vent about Jane and me.

This made me do some internal searching on my own and I found that I had a similar feeling. We have been a family of three for more than five years and each of us has created new personas. Each of us has found ways to cope with Conner's death and to become whole again. It isn't the same whole; we aren't the same people we were prior to the accident and we will never be those people again. We are, to differing degrees and to different realities, whole. The gaping wound has scarred over. We have revised what it means to be whole. We have learned how to adapt to this new life without Conner.

chapter thirteen
an irish wake

I wasn't dating anyone at the time so Conner was my "plus one" at my sister's wedding. He was determined to have as much fun as possible and to embarrass me as much as he could. He decided that the best way to accomplish both of those goals was to pretend to be my boyfriend.

Now my family knew Conner well and knew that neither of us was gay. None-theless, he would try and hold my hand and would sneak kisses to my cheek whenever I wasn't looking. My family laughed and understood that it was just Conner being Conner. The groom's family, on the other hand, was not quite sure what was going on.

-Jeff Polits

At one point on that first Sunday afternoon, I found a dozen of Conner's friends sprawled out around his room. They were talking and laughing and telling stories. It felt so completely comfortable and familiar. There were countless times when I had walked into his room to find him and his friends just hanging out and talking and laughing.

I sat and listened to a few of the stories and loved hearing their laughter. I came to realize, however, that this was their time to grieve, to grieve together as a group—a group that I wasn't a part of. I knew how they felt about me, I was the Old Man, the sometimes-intimidating, usually jovial, voice of authority. I was with them but not *of* them. Before I left, they told me how they had cleaned the pornography off of Conner's MacBook. I was pleased that they were doing that, not only to protect his memory, but also to protect Moira. It was their way of doing something for Conner that they knew he would have done for each of them. They explained that it was part of the "Bro Code."

Later that day, after the friends left his room but before it was time to go to the prayer vigil, I had the opportunity to lie on Conner's bed. While I could hear people talking in the backyard, I focused on smelling Conner's scent; it was in his bed and in his clothes still strewn around the room. I could feel his presence. I could harken back to that life that was only a few days passed. I could still feel what normalcy was like.

One matter that was starting to cause me some stress was that I had volunteered to give Conner's eulogy at the memorial mass scheduled for Tuesday evening. I had never given a eulogy before and, quite frankly, had not really listened to any of the eulogies that I had heard over the years. I was stumped and my initial enthusiasm was displaced by uncertainty. What do you say about a son who has died way too early? The death of a child is contrary to the usual order of things. I tried coming up with some sort of rationale for his death—some sort of justification but everything I tried was hackneyed and/or trite. This *wasn't* God's will. This *wasn't* all for the best. This *wasn't* just one of life's great mysteries. This just sucked but I couldn't say that.

I was stumped and my numerous attempts to sit at the computer and type resulted in nothing appropriate or even minimally adequate. Lying on Conner's bed that afternoon, surrounded by his clothes and scent, I tried not to think about the eulogy but just let my body relax. I closed my eyes and let my mind roam to wherever it wanted to go.

There have been only a few times in my life where instant inspiration came to me. Once I was in the middle of a trial when a sudden and new strategy allowed me to rescue victory from the jaws of defeat. Other times it was an idea to surprise someone that I loved or to buy a perfect gift. Lying there on Conner's bed, I had one of those epiphanies. Like a bolt out of the blue, I instantly knew the theme of the eulogy and, only moments later, I had it crafted in my mind. I knew exactly what I wanted to say and how I wanted to say it.

I ran down to the computer and started writing. It took me less than thirty minutes to write the entire eulogy. It seemed almost as if the eulogy wrote itself. Some might consider this to be some sort of divine inspiration or that I was channeling Conner's spirit. I have no idea if either of those may be true, but I do know that the eulogy came like a gift.

Now that I was finished writing it, it was time to worry about whether or not I was strong enough to stand up at the memorial mass and read it.

* * *

Preparing for the prayer vigil was peculiar; it still didn't feel as if Conner was dead. Moira left to join some friends and to share in the community of grieving teenagers. She needed to be around her friends, as well as Conner's, and they needed to be around her.

Jane and I showered and dressed, rarely talking or just making small talk. We drove to Jesuit High School, arriving shortly before the 7:00 p.m. start time.

I should mention at this point that Jesuit High School has a sprawling campus that is more like a small college than a high school. They have a large plaza between a few of the buildings and it was there that they set up chairs. Walking into the plaza, we were both pleased and surprised to see several hundred people there already—students, parents, friends, and faculty.

After various prayers, people stood and talked about Conner. Of course, there were tears and it was emotional but not for me. It was too surreal. I looked at a picture of Conner projected on the side of one of the buildings, but I had no emotional sense of him being dead. I could still feel his essence; he was still too alive to be dead. Intellectually, I knew the truth but as I looked at this picture of my boy—my son, I had no sense that I would never see him again. I had no ache in my stomach at his loss.

I was able to get up and thank everyone for coming to honor Conner. I shed no tears; my voice didn't crack. I even cracked a joke about one of Conner's favorite teachers. He wasn't really dead…at least not yet; at least not yet to me.

* * *

We had a semi-traditional Irish Wake for Conner without really meaning to. Every night for the first four nights, from that first Saturday night until the following Tuesday night, the night of his memorial mass, people gathered at our house to eat, drink, and tell stories. It was fun and the house was filled with laughter. None of it was planned and almost all of it was welcome. It was a spontaneous happening. People needed to gather and share their grief. Our home seemed like the most logical place to do so.

While the days were filled with sunshine, friends, and family—as well as brief glimpses of the real world—the nights were filled with drunken revelry. On Monday evening, a group of the boys got together and thought it would be a great idea to buy sex toys and bring them over. Jeff Polits, wearing a large black strap-on dildo, walked up to me and said, "K Dub, give me a hug!" Needless to say, I passed but I understood that by acting so outrageously, the boys were paying tribute to Conner and his own special brand of impropriety.

Another night, the woman who used to cut Conner's hair, Louise Botterill, re-created one of Conner's old exploits. A couple of years earlier, Conner had taken one of my old ties and, using White-Out, wrote on it, "My Cock is Huge!" He then proceeded to wear it from time to time to parties, solely for the shock value. When Jane and I saw it, we just rolled our eyes. We knew it wasn't that he was bragging, although we had no idea if he actually was well-endowed or if, alternatively, just engaging in a bit of truth inflation. We knew, however, that this was an example of Conner just being outrageous and loving the look of shock he could bring to people's faces. He didn't shock to offend; he shocked to laugh.

After a couple of months of seeing Conner's tie lying around his room, we figured that the joke had run its course and threw it away. With us now in full Irish-Wake mode, and with the boys pushing the boundaries of impropriety, Louise figured it was time to show that Conner's female friends could also be outrageous. She re-created the tie and gave it to us.

That same night, Conner's cousin Drew went out to pick up some more beer. He returned with a six-pack of Rogue Brewery's Dead Guy Ale. He knew that his cousin would have appreciated the humor of that gesture.

* * *

This was not a wake for the timid or the faint of heart. This was a full-on Irish Wake, full of love, laughter, and hijinks. It was a beautiful way to honor a beautiful boy. We all needed to show how important Conner was. His friends needed to be able to say goodbye. The fact that it was at our house—a house that they had spent countless hours at—was important because they needed the house, and us, as a touchstone. They needed us to be there, not only to remind them of Conner, but also as a reminder that not everything in their lives would change. Jane and I had become a second set of parents to a lot of these kids, and they wanted and needed to know that we were still there for them. Likewise, Jane and I desperately wanted to hold on to these relationships, as Conner was a part of each and every one of them.

Unfortunately, many of these relationships did fade over time. While we knew that this was inevitable, it wasn't welcome. We understood that while Conner's friends at twenty or twenty-three might still need us, they would eventually grow and form new relationships. The holes in their hearts left by Conner's death would gradually be filled with new friends and new memories. As they fell in love and matured, we would gradually fall out of their lives. This was natural and expected but, as it happened, it still hurt.

Over the coming years we learned that we weren't always a welcome presence, as we brought back painful memories or because we were no longer relevant. In doing research for this book, I interviewed a number of people, including an old friend of Conner's from the neighborhood—Hannah Frazier. I took her out to breakfast and we spent almost two hours talking about Conner. Hannah grew up only a block or so from our house, and she spent as much time at our home as Conner did at hers. We were always glad to come home and see Hannah at the kitchen counter, and it was sad when they started growing apart in high school.

At the end of our breakfast, Hannah invited us to her upcoming wedding. We accepted the invitation and the wedding was lovely. We didn't, however, go to the reception. This was to be Hannah's day and it should only be filled with joy. We knew that if we went to the reception, it would remind her that Conner wasn't there—where he should have been—to celebrate with her. We didn't want to be responsible for bringing up sad memories; we didn't want to do anything to detract from the joy of her wedding day. We were aware enough to know that the best gift we could give to Hannah was to congratulate her on her wedding and then disappear.

As the years progressed, we understood how we were treading a fine line with many of Conner's old friends. We could be a touchstone to remind them of what a great friend they once had, but we could not overstay our welcome. We were the past for most of these kids and had little, if any, relevance to their future. We became memories, sometimes joyful and other times painful. As with most memories, we began to fade from their lives.

* * *

There are certain practicalities that need to be addressed when someone dies. With both of my parents, we knew that the end was approaching, and we were able to make funeral arrangements in advance. When they finally passed away a couple of simple phone calls took care of everything.

With a sudden and unexpected death, that is not the case. In addition to dealing with my own grief, as well as that of Jane's and Moira's, I had issues to deal with—such as how to handle the replacement of the car. I had to argue with the insurance company as to the value of my totaled Saab. Perhaps I was grasping for anything to distract me from reality but, nonetheless, the haggling over the fair market value of the car that my son had died in seemed unseemly and disrespectful.

Of course, more important than all of that was the issue of what to do with Conner's body. As a result of the type of death, organ donation was not a possibility. We knew that the body had been horribly burned, so there was no discussion of any sort of open-casket viewing. Jane and I had long discussed that we both wanted to be cremated and have our ashes spread in various locales. The thought of rotting in a casket was repellant to both of us. Of course, there had never been any discussion about what Conner's and Moira's wishes might be.

After confirming with Jane and Moira that they agreed with me, I got online and tracked down a local crematorium. On Monday morning, I made the arrangements and they took care of everything. They arranged for the transportation of his body from the morgue to the crematorium. Later that week, they called me when it was time for me to pick up Conner's ashes. As I drove home, the plain white box containing my son's ashes sat on the seat beside me, the same seat that he had sat on countless times as we drove wherever. There was no comfort from that plain white box. There was no happiness emanating from that plain white box. There was no sense of "Conner" there. Rather, it was striking to imagine that the life, the joy, and the overwhelming vigor that had been Conner was now reduced to ash and now resided in that plain white box.

What a waste. Conner deserved so much more.

* * *

Driving to the memorial mass on Tuesday evening was surreal. We were focusing on how we looked and who we were going to see, anything to distract us from what the mass was really for. In some ways, the gravity and finality of the situation still hadn't sunk in, but it was starting to. We knew that the mass was a final opportunity for our friends and family to share a collective goodbye to Conner and to remember his life, but that wasn't what it felt like. We weren't ready to say goodbye to Conner. We weren't even ready to acknowledge, to honestly acknowledge in our hearts, that he was really gone forever. It was still too soon. Even now, we're still not ready.

The memorial mass was held at Jesuit High School's theater and we got there a bit early and started to greet people. You could see that some people were uncomfortable talking to us, and we tried to put them at ease by giving them a hug and a smile. We were relaxed, and not solely from the medications we were all on. It was all so surreal and keeping ourselves detached from the grief allowed us to function almost as gracious hosts.

I gazed up at the stage and there was a large picture of Conner on an easel to the side of the altar. He looked so handsome and alive. We were pleased to see so many people there, all to show their respect for Conner and the rest of us. There were friends, classmates, work colleagues, neighbors, and many people we didn't recognize.

The three of us—Jane, Moira and myself—sat down in the front row, surrounded by Jane's family and mine, as well as most of Conner's closest friends. When the mass started, I allowed my mind to wander. I stopped listening to the priest and just started thinking. I thought back to a time, only slightly more than six years prior, when there had been a prayer vigil in that very same venue for one of Conner's classmates. Just a week after their freshman year, Conner's friend Brett Davies committed suicide. His death came as a complete shock to everyone and hit Conner hard, as he had been over to Brett's house only the day before.

Jesuit High School, in all of its institutional wisdom, immediately scheduled a prayer vigil to allow the students and their families to mourn Brett as a community. We were seated on the side of the theater and about two-thirds of the way up. I remember looking down at the Davies family. I saw Brett's parents and his two siblings. They were all dressed in black and appeared near-catatonic. I watched them with an almost morbid curiosity, not knowing how someone deals with the death of a child. I remember pitying them and thinking to myself, "Oh, those poor Davies."

The night of Conner's memorial mass, I let my mind's eye travel up to those exact seats and look down at the now-grieving family, this time not the Davies, but us. I knew exactly what the people sitting in those seats could see. I could see how we looked from behind—dressed in black, appearing near-catatonic. I knew what these people were thinking: "Oh, those poor Lubys."

Finally, it was time for me to take the stage and give Conner's eulogy. I had printed it out, using a larger font size since I didn't want to have to squint to see the words. Apparently, the larger font size still wasn't large enough. I hadn't taken into account the fact that I would be crying so much and so unabashedly. This is what I read, or at least tried to read:

Let me share with you what I believe. I believe that everyone has a purpose in life. Death is a tragedy only when that purpose goes unfulfilled. Some of us may know what our purpose is but, I suspect, that most of us don't... not for sure. One's purpose only becomes clear as time goes by and even then, may only truly become clear through the shadow of death and, even then, not to ourselves but to those who survive us.

Conner certainly had a purpose. I believe that his purpose was to bring joy to others. His purpose was to make others laugh, to be there when friends needed him. His purpose was to live his life to the fullest and the loudest and to touch as many lives as he could. He pursued this purpose by being outrageous, loving, annoying, considerate, frustrating, funny, compassionate and, in almost all things, completely inappropriate. He just had a good heart.
Reluctantly, I have to believe that he succeeded in fulfilling his purpose.

My belief is reluctant because it was for such a short period of time and ended so swiftly and so unexpectedly. The tough thing for us, those left behind, is to wonder why his purpose couldn't have been more. Why, rather than being here for less than twenty-one years, his purpose couldn't have been to be here for thirty or forty years or more and spread more joy?

As his father, I selfishly wanted his purpose to be to live much longer, to let me see him fall in love…the way I fell in love with his mother. To let me see him get married and celebrate twenty-five amazing years…just as Jane and I have. To let me see him become a father—to hold a newborn child, my grandchild, in his hands and realize that he had just helped create a new life. To let me see him stumble and bumble and make mistakes with his kids…just like I did. To let him experience so many of the joys and frustrations that I have had the great fortune to experience with Conner and Moira. And trust me, I wouldn't trade a single one of those joys or frustrations.

I wanted his purpose to be to let me help him become the man, the husband, and the father that I always wanted him to be. Unfortunately, that is not to be and I reluctantly have to accept that his purpose, his true purpose in life, is something other than what I wanted for him.

Over the last several days, I heard so many stories, have seen so many tears, and have felt so much love that I truly, truly believe that Conner fulfilled his purpose. So this is not a tragedy despite the pain I feel in my heart. This is not a tragedy because Conner did bring joy; he was there when his friends needed him…and he had a lot of friends. He did live life to the fullest and the loudest, albeit for a very, very short time.

On behalf of my wife Jane, I want to thank you for all of your love and support. The amount of time and effort that you, our friends and family, have given to us, has been remarkable. I don't know how, and even whether, we would have made it through without you.

On behalf of Moira, who is experiencing something that no sixteen year old should ever have to experience, I want to thank you. Her friends have come to her side and have been so supportive – thank you Leanna, Natalie, Calvin, Sara, Cassie, Sadie and everyone else who has been there for her.

I also want to note something that has become amazingly clear in the last couple of days. That is that Conner was not Moira's only sibling. Megan Mac, you could not be more of a sister to her, or a daughter to us, than you are. Thank you.

Of her brothers, I want to mention just a few…Jon, Jeff, Alex, Marcus, Logan, Big Mike, Jason….you have big shoes to fill but I know you will. And I want to remind you of one of the biggest obligations that big brothers have…to beat the crap out of anyone who breaks their little sister's heart.

I believe that I am right, that Conner has fulfilled the purpose for which he was placed in this world. While I wish he could have had more, while I wish that I could have had more, I am grateful for the time we had with him and I will always, always love him.

I have two favors to ask of each of you. First, if you have any stories about, or photos of, Conner, please share them with us…at least those that aren't too wildly inappropriate.

Secondly, and more importantly, for Conner's sake and in Conner's memory, live a wonderful life. Let Conner's life and love shine through you. Live a wonderful life. He did.

I took a moment to gather my papers but, in reality, I was trying to gather my wits and regain my composure. Again, it was time for me to put the mask back on. It was time for me to push my grief to the back of my mind and provide comfort to friends and family.

The mass ended to the sound of Irish bagpipers playing "Amazing

Grace." We followed the bagpipers out and then stayed a while to console and be consoled.

Afterwards, we invited people back to our house for the final night of the Irish Wake. Some came; most didn't. I understood that some people couldn't be around us. I knew that the frivolity of an Irish Wake was too jarring for many. More than anything else, however, I knew that this was to be our last night to fend off the finality. I knew that the next day was the start of the next stage of our lives.

At the end of the night, after the last friend left, we were alone – just the three of us. The days of running around for the Irish Wake and memorial service were over. The chaos that we had embraced in order to keep the grief at bay was over. It was time for our families to go home to their lives and for friends to get on with theirs. We knew that it was now our time to adapt to, and accept, the new reality. It was time to let the fact that Conner was really gone sink in.

That evening, September 15, 2009, while we were saying our public goodbyes to Conner, Jane and I should have been celebrating our twenty-fifth wedding anniversary. The anniversary passed with little more than a hollow "Happy Anniversary," whispered to one another as we held each other in the dark and slowly fell asleep.

* * *

In the days that followed, the sun rose and the sun set. Moira eventually returned to school and Jane and I returned to work. The sun rose and the sun set. We still didn't know exactly what had happened that evening—September 12, 2009. We still didn't know why Conner died. We could speculate; we could guess; we could place blame. At the end of the day, however, it didn't really matter. Conner wasn't coming back, no matter who or what was to blame. It just didn't matter but, soon enough, it would.

chapter fourteen
mancakes

The one thing I can always remember is how, if he wanted something, he went for it. Whether that was being the funny kid on the playground trying to make all the girls laugh or begging me to let him see my booklet of "girl parts" after sex-ed. Such a little shit, haha, but how could you not love him and how persistent he was?!?

All he cared about was making someone smile. This is what keeps me going every day. I miss him each day and I can honestly say that I'm a better person because I knew him.

-Hannah Frazier

Out of sheer coincidence, late summer and the fall have always been incredibly busy for our family. In addition to the start of school, there was Halloween, which we always went overboard on. There was our wedding anniversary and the October birthdays of Moira and Conner, followed shortly thereafter by the November birthdays of Jane and me. Then came Thanksgiving and Christmas. Mixed in with all of those events were sports practices and games. It seemed as if every week was chock-full of activity.

Conner's death might cast a pall on some of these happenings but it couldn't stop them. Moira's seventeenth birthday was to be the first of these events after Conner's death. We were determined to try and bring some joy to her. Accordingly, we went overboard. We invited a large group of friends—some of them Moira's, some of them Conner's—and went to Professional Bull Riding. Afterward, we came home for cake and presents. We spoiled Moira rotten. At the end of the night, before everyone left, we broke out some Irish whiskey and toasted Conner. The frivolity was as forced as it was necessary.

Only three weeks later, it was Conner's birthday—his twenty-first birthday. As we had been told to do by our grief counselor, we invited friends to surround us to help "celebrate" Conner's birthday.

We scheduled two separate celebrations. The first was a birthday breakfast at the Stepping Stone Café in Portland. Conner had long told us that on his twenty-first birthday, he wanted to go there for "mancakes." These are disgustingly large pancakes. Local family, as well as friends of Conner's and ours, joined us. All together there were about twenty of us.

Two of Conner's friends, Jeff Polits and Jason Tumpane, decided to take the mancake challenge. The Café has a challenge that if you can eat three mancakes in one sitting, you get your picture up on the wall. Jeff and Jason went *mano a mano* and both successfully completed the challenge. Letting my sadistic streak come to the fore, I summoned all of the pomp and authority that I could manage and proclaimed that finishing the mancakes was only the first part of the challenge. The second part required them to race around the block.

Whether from exhaustion or emotional numbness, both of them agreed. They took off on a sprint and the rest of us walked to the far end of the block to wait for them. Impressively, Jason (formerly known as Leukie Boy), somehow came sprinting around the corner minutes later looking none the worse for wear. Jeff, however, was nowhere to be seen. We went looking for him and he was waddling back to the Café, his face alternating between pale white and green. We called out to him to encourage him and he tried to smile back at us. All of a sudden, he turned into someone's driveway, leaned over and deposited most of the undigested mancakes in the bushes. It wasn't pretty but it was pretty funny.

The second birthday event was dinner at Chili's Restaurant for chicken fried steak. I wish I could explain why our family has such an affinity for that dish. We know it isn't healthy but, when properly prepared, it is as close to culinary heaven as we can find. Conner had been adamant that he wanted chicken fried steak for dinner on his twenty-first birthday. That is what we did for him.

While at dinner, we asked Jon Pelzer to take the ceremonial shot of Irish whiskey for Conner. It seemed apropos since they were such long-time friends, and Jon was more than up to the challenge. After dinner, we took a group photo and then disbursed into the night, the three of us returning to our all-too-quiet and empty home. There would be no discarded gift wrapping strewn around the floor. There would be no leftover cake in the kitchen. There was just the three of us, each of us lost in our own private thoughts.

* * *

We knew that the Oregon State Police were conducting an investigation into the accident, just as they did with every traffic fatality. We would check in with the investigating trooper from time to time throughout the fall to see how things were progressing. It was more than idle curiosity; we were still searching for some explanation. Personally, I was still looking for someone to blame. I wanted the report to prove that the truck driver had been negligent and was responsible for my son's death. I wanted justice for Conner.

The trooper called me one afternoon in November to ask if he could come by my office that evening to give me the final report. I called Jane and she and Moira came to my office so that we could all hear the report together. The trooper explained some of the basics and confirmed that Conner had died instantly and that there was a positive identification. He then paused and somberly told us that the toxicology report came back and showed that Conner had been drunk at the time of the accident. He explained that Conner's blood alcohol content was 0.17%, more than twice the legal limit.

For the first time since the accident, I was angry, really angry. I was irate; I was enraged...I was pissed. Conner knew better than to drink and drive! What the hell was he thinking? I knew that Conner, in the past, had taken keys away from friends whom he knew shouldn't be driving. I knew that Conner had walked home from parties before because he knew that he had been drinking. What the hell was he thinking? He knew better.

The trooper saw the emotions raging inside of me and looked me in the eye and answered the question that I had not yet asked. He said, "He was a kid and he made a stupid mistake. That's what kids do."

I felt my shoulders sag as my anger dissipated as quickly as it had appeared.

Was that really it? Was that the only explanation? Was it so simple as to be that he was just a kid and that he made a stupid mistake? How could my son be dead solely because of that simple explanation? How could all of this grief be caused by something as simple as a mistake?

As much as I didn't want to, I knew that it was the truth and that I had to accept it. The momentary anger was displaced by the return of the grief, the scab again ripped off violently. With only a minor hesitation, but because Jane and Moira were there, I slipped the mask back on. I comforted them and told them none of this news changed the way we felt about Conner. I reaffirmed that we still loved him. Nothing anyone else could say would ever change how we felt about him. He was just a kid and had made a stupid mistake and he was now gone. It was as simple as that. He was, however, still our son and Moira's brother and nothing could ever change that.

In the days that followed, as I read and re-read the police report in the solitude of my office, the mask would slip away. At such times, I would alternate between brief bouts of anger and then lengthy episodes of painful despair. The fact that Conner had just been a kid and made a stupid mistake provided little, if any, real comfort. From an intellectual standpoint I understood it, and this information certainly assuaged my anger, but I found no real comfort in it. It just wasn't right; it just wasn't fair.

* * *

In the months following receipt of the accident report, Jane began to wonder about the truck driver and how he was dealing with the accident. She knew that as difficult as this had been for us, it must have also been difficult for him. She sensed that even though we now knew he wasn't responsible, he was likely still feeling both guilt and grief. This was the type of inherent empathy that Conner had learned from her.

Her curiosity about the well-being of the driver became stronger and stronger, as did the feeling that she needed to reach out to him. Jane felt as if Conner was pushing her to do what he would have wanted her to do—what he certainly would have done if he could. The compulsion increased daily. We had learned the driver's name from the accident report, and Jane finally tracked down his phone number.

It was after the holidays and Jane just called him one afternoon. He seemed wary at first but Jane told him that she just wanted to make sure that he was okay and to thank him for his efforts in trying to put out the fires. She told him that she harbored no anger at him and, in fact, understood that Conner's death must have taken an emotional toll on him also.

The driver started to cry and told Jane that a day didn't pass without him thinking about the accident. While he had never gone online to see Conner's Facebook page, his wife had and she told him about the impact that Conner's death had had on so many people. His wife told him what a handsome boy Conner had been. And still, he could not allow himself to look at any pictures of Conner.

Jane could tell that his involvement in the accident was crushing his spirit. Even though he had not done anything wrong, he had been involved in an accident that resulted in the death of much-loved young man. He felt guilt and constantly wondered whether or not he could have done something, whether he should have been looking more carefully for oncoming traffic.

Jane let him know that we didn't blame him at all and that we truly regretted that he had to be involved. She told him that she wished him well and that she hoped he could have a great life.

Just before they ended their conversation, the truck driver asked Jane a peculiar question. He told her that he had been having dreams about the accident and that the dreams always involved four stars. He asked her whether that had any significance, and Jane explained that Conner had had a tattoo of four stars on his chest.

chapter fifteen
palancas

Cut back to sophomore year of high school, and Erin comes up to me and says, "Hey, Conner Luby's looking for you." All I can think is …are you kidding me? This has got to be a joke. Either the man-whore wants a challenge or Erin confused her Megans. Ten minutes later, up waltzes Conner, "Hey. You seem like a cool chick, can I chill for a bit?" And so it began, as simply as that.

The next Monday we were grabbing lunch together and I informed him that despite the fact that he was straight, he would, henceforth, be my Jack from Will & Grace. Done and done. And thus, he became "Poodle."

Starting there, we were amongst the weirdest set of best friends that anyone could have paired together. We make absolutely no sense if you know us separately, but as soon as you see the two of us together it works. We're like magic. There's something so quirky and weird about the way we click, it can only be captured in the words of Tennessee Williams: "Any true thing between two people is too rare to be normal."

-Megan McAninch

While Jesuit High School was expensive, I will never regret having sent Conner there. It introduced him to so much, and to so many, and truly helped shape the man he was, as well as the man he was becoming. The Jesuit High School community provided great strength and support throughout our difficult times, and many of my closest friends remain Jesuit parents.

One aspect of Jesuit High School that I particularly enjoyed, albeit from a distance, was the Junior Encounter—formally known as the

April Co-Ed Encounter and, informally, as "ACE." The high school hosted annual retreats for each of the classes and, while they were not mandatory, attendance was strongly encouraged. This was considered to be an opportunity for the kids to review their spiritual beliefs and to bond with their classmates outside of the confines of ordinary high school life. The Junior Encounter is considered to be the most special.

One of the activities of the Junior Encounter is to encourage friends and family members to write to the students, give encouragement, and express their love for the students, without pretense and without reservation. These letters are called "palancas," which basically mean letters of encouragement.

This is the big secret of the Junior Encounter, as the students don't find out about them until it is time to read them. Accordingly, the palancas generally come from family members, faculty, and seniors. We couldn't let Moira write a palanca to Conner because it would have ruined the surprise for her when her time came to participate in her Junior Encounter.

Jane and I both wrote palancas to Conner. For mine, I took advantage of having a relatively captive audience to give Conner the type of lecture he otherwise never would have sat still for.

April 24, 2006

Conner,

One of the toughest things about being a parent is that there is no real reference or instruction manual that you can rely upon. In raising you and your sister, your mother and I relied upon the examples set by our parents. Unfortunately for you, your grandparents were deeply flawed. Fortunately for you, we are not.

We have distilled our experiences and used them to figure out how to be your parents. Clearly, some things that our parents did, they did very well and helped turn us into the people that we are. We also look at the things that your grandparents didn't do very well and try to avoid those. We have, however, had mixed success with this.

Grandpa Luby was very sarcastic and I always hated that. It was only later, after you and your sister were born, that I came to learn how effective, and fun, sarcasm can be. Accordingly, sarcasm will remain one of my favorite parenting tools.

Similarly, your mother has retained some of the attributes of her parents but we won't get into that here.

In any event, the learning process of becoming a parent is similar to how you learned to read—guess and go. Sometimes the guesses work out and sometimes not. This is one of the reasons why we sometimes refer to you as "The Grand Experiment."

There is no doubt that we have made our share of mistakes in raising you. Please know, however, that all of these mistakes were made with deep love and for all of the right reasons. We have, over the years, given you a lot of freedom and this may have been a mistake. Our thinking, however, was that we trust you and believe that your strong sense of right and wrong will keep you out of trouble. Further, we figured that you wouldn't grow and mature unless you were given the opportunity to make your decisions. It's tough for us, however, to see you make mistakes when we could have told you the right way to do things. You don't learn as well, though, when we tell you something. Sometimes experience really is the best teacher.

Over the course of the last seventeen plus years, you have made mistakes…a lot of mistakes. The good news is that none of the mistakes have been uncorrectable. The bad news is that you will continue to make mistakes for the rest of your life. That's what people do…they make mistakes. It's just a part of life. The problem is not making mistakes. The problem with mistakes is when people repeat them and fail to learn from them and keep repeating the same patterns and mistakes over and over again. Let me give you an example…your hair looks like crap. It is a mistake. Learn from this.

Over the next several years, you will continue the process of achieving independence. Remember, however, that independence carries both freedom and responsibility. As the great philosopher Uncle Ben from Spiderman once said, "With great power comes great responsibility." One of the things we've begun talking about is your responsibility to the Family...not to just do what is asked of you, but also to do what needs to be done without even being asked. Be aware of your surroundings. Look around. Does the lawn need to be mowed? If so, then mow it. Don't wait for me to mention it to you. Do the animals need to be fed? If so, do it. Don't wait for me to ask. Does the bathroom need a new roll of toilet paper? You get the idea.

The responsibilities to the Family will next expand into your responsibility to the Community. Does someone need help? Help them. Don't wait for them to ask. Do people need blood? Donate. Don't wait for the Red Cross to call you. Is there a charity that you can help? The answer is yes. Find a charity that "clicks" with you and get involved. Community involvement sometimes requires you to work a bit harder in that you need to be active and not just reactive. This is what it means to be a responsible adult and a member of the Community. This is what it means to be a leader and not just a follower.

One of my greatest, and possibly my only, disappointment about you is that I sense that you are afraid to do your best. Perhaps you think that if you do your best and it is still not good enough, you will be judged a failure. Perhaps you prefer to be thought of as someone with great potential rather than what you really are. If so, this will prevent you from ever realizing your potential. Don't you want to find out what is really possible for you? Maybe you're capable of great things; maybe not. Maybe it depends upon your definition of great things. I have no doubt that you are capable of so much more than you think you are. You just need to find out. Failure is not a problem as long as you try your best. Failure is only a problem when you give up before giving it your best.

Let me give you an example. I want to win this election but I know that there is a significant chance that I won't. Should I have avoided the whole process in order to avoid having some people think I'm a loser? If I lose, will I be any less of a person? One thing I know is that if I do lose, it won't be from a lack of trying.

I realize that I will likely never make the front page of the New York Times or the cover of Time magazine. I'll never win an Oscar, a

Grammy, an Emmy, a Pulitzer or Nobel Prize. I will never be voted People Magazine's Sexiest Man. I'll never fly to outer space or climb Mt. Everest. I'll never be President of the United States or be the world's richest man. So what. Let me tell you what I have accomplished. I have met, romanced, married, and remained married to the love of my life. I have fathered (I think!) and raised two great kids. I have laughed at myself and experienced amazing amounts of happiness. I have failed at things too numerous to count but never regretted trying. I have accomplished great things. I have screwed up but learned from it. You can too.

Do your best at whatever you do. Don't worry about whether you are "successful" or not. If you experience happiness, you are successful. If you are a good person, you are successful. If you help others, you are successful. Your mother and I will be happy even if you are only a fry cook at McDonald's, as long as that is what you want to do and that you are happy. Find out what you are capable of. It makes the rest of life so much easier than if you're always afraid to try things because you might fail. Failure is just a part of learning and is an acceptable part of life (although not an acceptable part of your academic life!). We have always been more proud of effort than of results.

Your Mom and I will always love you. Even when you screw up and we get pissed off, we love you. There is nothing you could ever do that would stop us from loving you. There may be times when we don't like you, but we will always love you. As you become an adult and eventually have your own family, learn from us. The things we've done well, continue to do. The mistakes that we've made, avoid repeating. It's not that tough.

I am so proud of the man you are becoming. It's almost like looking in the mirror...except that you have hair. I love you.

> *The Old Man*
> *aka Dad*
> *aka Your Hero*
> *aka Your Role Model*
> *aka Abdul*

Before setting out Jane's palanca, you should know that a popular movie at that time was *10 Things I Hate About You*. Jane, with some creative assistance from me, used that title as her inspiration. She never would have said anything like this to Conner if she was serious and, at all times, had her tongue planted firmly in her cheek.

To: *Conner*

From: *Mom*

Re: *10 Things I Hate About You*

1. You're a slob. How can you possibly stand to live in that cesspool you call your room. It smells like boy. Can't you smell it? How can you sleep night-after-night, week-after-week in the same sheets with all of those boy germs and who knows what else? Yuck!

2. What's up with your hair? Could it be that you are convinced that you will someday look like your father and want to enjoy long hair as long as you can? Hmmm...that might be a good idea but can't we at least cut the split ends? Your father is starting to worry about you because of all the product you put in your hair. I have assured him that he has nothing to worry about and that you are a committed heterosexual. I am right, aren't I?

3. Your driving! OK, so this may be the pot calling the kettle black but of all my attributes, you had to copy my driving skills? Couldn't you have copied my culinary skills? Or my youthful appearance? Or my patience and even temper?

4. Fear of Commitment. So who's the flavor of the week now? No wonder we confused Amber with Sami with Jenny with Tiffany with Jessica with Jackie (Grrr!) with Nichole with Michelle with ??? How the hell do you keep them all straight? Is there a problem with settling down with a single girl...at least for a week or two? I'm not talking marriage

*but it might be nice to see you with the same girl two times in a row. I
know, you're looking for a girl just like your dear old Ma. Keep looking,
there aren't many like me but when you find someone like me, the search
will be well worth it.*

*5. Your eating habits! I thought it was bad when you made that ground
beef and egg concoction but, Good Lord, you eat more crap than anyone
I have ever known. Potato chip quesadillas? I realize that you have a fast
metabolism but it will eventually slow down. After all, your father used to
have a fast metabolism too and look what's happened to him. You need to
start eating healthier. Your body is like an engine and it needs good fuel.
Whether or not you pursue athletics, you will avoid colds, the flu and other
illnesses by eating healthier. Remember, vegetables can be your friends.
Plus, the girls really dig guys who eat healthy.*

*6. Academics. Hello, is there anybody home? Have you noticed how
you start every semester by digging yourself a big hole and then having
to scramble out of it? Have you noticed how it's always the teachers that
misplaced your homework or made a mistake grading it? How is it that
you've had the misfortune of having 11 years worth of teachers that can't
keep track of homework that you've handed in? What's worse is that they
appear to single you out and rarely lose anyone else's homework. Why is
that?*

*You may think that we push academics so that you can get into college
and have a great and successful life. Actually, we think of the benefits as
you going off to college and being successful enough to be able to take care
of your father and me in our old age. Maybe I'm just being selfish but you
owe me. You can't imagine the pain I went through to give birth to you.
It's because of you, and that scar from the Caesarian section, that I had
to give up my dream of being a nude model. Yes, you owe me and you owe
me big. Start studying so that you can repay your debt.*

7. Your phone skills. What do you mean that you never check your messages? Why is it that you rarely, if ever, answer the phone when I call? I used to complain when the only problem was your inability to take phone messages. You're regressing not progressing.

8. Sagging Pants. Let me make this perfectly clear. NO ONE WANTS TO SEE YOUR UNDERWEAR. This is not a good look for you. You don't need to wear khakis and golf shirts but, please, at least pull up your pants.

9. Excuses. Your tried-and-true method when confronted with mistakes is to immediately look to shift the blame. If I start chastising you for crapping out the bathroom, you immediately respond with "…but this is Moira's mess too!" One of these days you'll learn that it is much easier, and more mature, to stay focused on how you screwed up, apologize and then move on. That will hopefully come with maturity, which now leads us to Number 10.

10. Maturity. OK, so there are two kinds of maturity. Physical maturity is not a problem. You have obviously matured into a man and I don't want to think about that any further. Emotional maturity, however, is still a work in progress. Emotional maturity consists of things such as responsibility, pride and empathy.

Emotional maturity involves acknowledging your mistakes, and that your actions do have consequences, some of which may not have been anticipated. Saying that "I didn't mean to…" doesn't solve the problem. Maturity involves not just recognizing the mistake and apologizing for it but also doing what is necessary and right so as to address the results of your mistake.

While pride may be one of the seven deadly sins, it is also a sign of maturity. It is the pride in doing something well, or at least as well as you can. For far too long you've thought that good enough is good enough. With maturity comes the recognition that good enough isn't. You can only get by with mediocrity for so long. At some point, you need to do your best and find out how good your best is.

Empathy is the ability to put yourself in someone else's shoes—to be able to recognize that others are not as fortunate as you. Recognizing that someone is hurting and then trying to help comes with maturity. This is something you already have in spades and for that I am so proud.

Despite your obvious and numerous flaws, I do love you even though you really piss me off sometimes. You are a lucky boy to have someone as nice, patient and pretty as me for your mom. You had better appreciate it...and start paying up. I love you.

XOXO Mommio
aka Mommy Dearest
aka Colleen

In hindsight, these letters might not have met the true intent of a palanca. Rather than using this as an opportunity to just praise him and tell him how much we loved him, we chose to use this as a forum to counsel and lecture. Had we had the chance to do it again, we might have taken a different approach.

When it was Moira's turn for her to attend ACE in the Spring of 2009, Conner labored long and hard to come up with the perfect palanca for her, knowing that his parents were preparing their own treatises for her. He had a deep love for his little sister despite the fact that he often considered her to be the stereotypical annoying little sister. Conner could be, in turn, protective and dismissive of Moira, as well as proud and embarrassed. One year Moira was playing classic soccer and her team was playing in a tournament. We, as a family, were on the sidelines cheering her on. The game ended in a 3-3 tie. The teams then went into a shootout with five players from each team getting a chance to score. None of them did.

It then came time for the next set of five players from each team, Moira being the last. Just before her turn, a player from the other team scored so it was then up to Moira. If she missed, the game was over.

On the sidelines, all three of us held hands, as well as our breaths, as she prepared to shoot. We were stunned to see her blast a shot into the top, right-hand corner of the goal. Conner leaped high into the air and let out a scream. He then bounced out to the middle of the field where Moira was being congratulated by her teammates and gave her a big hug and told her how proud he was of her.

The fact that Moira's team eventually lost the game became little more than a footnote to this memory. Seeing her succeed and then seeing how proud Conner was of her, so completely and unabashedly, is what is important about the memory. Despite the various brother-sister spats we saw throughout the years, we never had any doubt how much he loved his little sister and how proud he was of her. This assurance is based, in part, upon the palanca that he wrote to her.

The morning the palancas were due, Conner came bounding into the kitchen boasting about the great palanca that he had written. He was so very excited to be able to share something like this with his little sister. He seemed to sense that this was a special opportunity to express his true feelings to his sister; an opportunity to tell his sister how much he truly loved her.

This is what Conner wrote to Moira:

> *Moira, my darling little shit of a sister,*
>
> *Bet you weren't expecting this, huh? You may have known about the letters from Mom and Dad's lack of ability to be secretive, but did you ever expect you'd have so many palancas?*
>
> *I think that's what they're called still. I'm not sure if I spelled it right, but its' been 3 years so give me a break. Oh, and periodically through this letter, I will go off on these random side notes because: A) the more I space out this letter and make it appear longer, the more you'll think I actually love you, or something like that. And B) because I just got home from an exhausting night of work and I forgot to take my Adderall today!!*
>
> *OK, so back to this whole palancas/cookies/whatever crazy terms you darn kids have come up with. I wonder who has more letters, me or you?!*

I'm gonna swallow my pride and say most likely it's you. Don't get me wrong, I was super rad back in my day so I had an impressive stack of letters but I think the fact that you have something called morals (whatever that is!) and you tend to not burn bridges as much as I did (cuz I'm perfect now) gives you the edge.

When you finished your big group chit-chat and whatever teacher or senior told you that you'll be going to your room for an hour and a half to meditate/reflect I know EXACTLY what was going through your head. "Finally! An hour and a half to 'reflect,' screw that! They made us get up at the ass crack of dawn, we had to get on that bus that took forever, we finally got here and I was starving and do I get to eat? Nooooo! I had to wait until after the big group talk, then the little group talk, THEN I got food! But wait, do I get any down time? NOPE! Another big group crying sesh. I'm drained, screw this, I'm napping!" So Moira, how's that nap coming along?

Here's a fun fact for ya: On my encounter I was roommates with Kevin McShane. Trainer Jen was the chaperone on my floor and knowing me and how even though this time is supposed to be a personal, independent thing, I'd still probably talk to Kevin and once again not follow the rules. So what did good ol' TJ do? Once I saw the big envelope on my bed, she made me follow her…then she put me in the storage closet by myself! (I was gonna add "lol" after that but, seeing as I didn't find it funny back then nor do I find it funny now so I'll skip the online lingo and you can laugh at my traumatizing events since I'm not there).

OK, wow, I really should have taken my Adderall before undertaking this little message. I can't focus to save my life!!! I really can't wait until Sunday when you're back and know all the secrets. Oh that's right, there's more than just this one! How are your small groups going? Have you cried yet? Don't worry if you haven't yet, believe me you will.

Once again, another side note. In my first small group I had GP (that's right, Mean Gene) and a bunch of people I knew but wasn't close with. I remember on the bus ride down telling everyone I wasn't gonna cry cuz I'm a bad A_ MO-FU!!! Wanna take a guess what happened? If you were to guess that by the end of the first small group that I'd be the FIRST person out of my group to cry, you'd be right. I didn't just cry, I bawled...seriously like borderline blubbering, no joke!!

So back to my questions, that I won't get answers to until you're back on Sunday. Big question, how stoked were you when you finally got to eat!?! Food is bomb, huh?! Oh, and the Tang is just the icing on the cake, my friend. How bummed were you after everyone telling you how many cookies you were gonna get and then you found out, in fact, there are no cookies, there's a stack of letters in an ugly manila envelope with the sole purpose of making you cry until your face is chapped!!! Letters are cool and all, but seriously when I found out I wasn't gonna be cramming 8000 calories worth of cookies down my throat everyday for an entire weekend it pretty much ruined my weekend (KIDDING).

Alright, enough with asking you the questions I already know the answers to. I mean, hey, I went through the exact same thing you are right now, and you are my little sister so you can't be too different! This is where I give you advice. I know I've only genuinely given you advice from the heart a couple of times, but I have two bits of good news! This happens to be one of those times, and now you're gonna have it written down so if you ever forget you can always just read this letter again! So here we go:

1) Don't be afraid. Your encounter is the time when you don't hold anything back. You may feel uncomfortable telling some of your classmates and teachers your deepest secrets and stories but you never have to worry about that. What is said in the small groups NEVER will get out. In my small group I learned some things about my classmates that I will never tell anyone. It may seem like a big risk, opening up and being vulnerable to your peers, but I promise that if you do, it will be one of the most rewarding experiences of your life.

2) Talk to some of your classmates that you rarely talk with or maybe haven't talked to ever. All your leaders will tell you to do this and I really can't stress it enough, TALK TO NEW PEOPLE! You may think that a person has nothing in common with you because they look different, are in a different group, or just don't seem interesting but, believe me, out of the few people I still talk to from high school, over half were people I hadn't talked to before I went on my encounter.

3) Take everything seriously. If you try and make everything a joke or you don't put everything you can into the activities, you'll waste your encounter and regret it down the road. With the encounter you'll get out of it as much as you're willing to put into it. I'm challenging you to put even more into yours than I did mine. LISTEN TO THE RIVER. Take a walk around St. Benny's by yourself and just notice what an amazing place it is.

The rest you can figure out for yourself. I'm not trying to give you a rulebook on how to do your encounter, I'm just trying to give you some ideas for things that might make your weekend a little bit more special. This is YOUR encounter. People aren't gonna look at you as Conner's little sister and see if you're doing it exactly like I did. This weekend is all about you, and discovering who you are as a person. If you realize you don't like something about yourself, change it. If you realize you've lost a friendship that you really want back, do what it takes to make amends. If you have a realization about your faith, follow your heart. This weekend's purpose is to open your eyes and think about yourself in a way you may never have before. It's going to be an emotional rollercoaster where you will remember events in your life that made you extremely sad, or people who may have started untrue rumors about you that made you insecure, or your closest friends that at one time or another did or said something that just broke you down. Out of all that sadness, I swear that you are going to experience amazing highs. It's inevitable that by the time you leave St. Benedicts, the 40 or so classmates you came down with will become some of your closest and most trusted friends. I can't tell you much about all the other good stuff that's going to happen to you without giving away all the good secrets, but what I can tell you is that no matter what, you're going to come back home the happiest and the most peaceful that you've ever been. I'm sure Mom is going to appreciate that!

Moira, you and I have never really gotten along. In fact one might

*say that we've been each others' nemesis for 16, going on 17, years. (I'm
counting from when you were born because even though I've been told that
I liked you back then, I don't remember it so I'm going to assume it's all
lies!!! Ha) I'm not gonna say that I've done everything wrong and I wish
I could go back and fix it all because I was a total jerk and you were
a princess that never did me any wrong. The fact is we've both treated
each other with such a low level of respect that it's impossible that we
could have gotten close. I realize how selfish I've been by not trying to
find out more about you, what you like, what you do for fun, why you
like such terrible TV shows, and so on and so forth. Here's something
I bet you didn't know: Every time I told you that you should go on the
Junior Encounter, it was because I really wanted us to have something this
important in common. We really don't see eye-to-eye on too many things,
but by Sunday, you'll understand truly how happy I am that we both went
on the Encounter. Think about it, all your classmates have already gone
on their encounters, which means more letters for you! I always felt bad
for October and November because who's gonna write them letters? That's
right, parents, teachers, and seniors. Maybe I'm wrong but that doesn't
sound nearly as good as getting tons of letters from people in your class.
Ever since you told me that you were going to be going on ACE like me,
as much as you may not have noticed, I've been a lot more patient with
you. I'm not saying every moment you annoy me, but little things like not
replacing the toilet paper, or taking my stuff without asking (or just not
returning it for that matter!), I didn't get nearly as upset as I did before
I knew what encounter you chose. The reason why is very simple. I know
that when you get back from this weekend, we're both going to realize we
have more in common than we ever could have thought. Just writing this
letter to you is bringing back so many memories, the feelings I felt, how my
attitude on life was completely changed, the compassion I developed, and
the desire to be a better person. When you get home, all the little stuff we've
fought about won't matter anymore. All the petty arguments over food, the
TV, or any material thing will all disappear. That is why I've been calmer
recently. It's because I knew that eventually this weekend would come and*

finally we could have a deeper relationship than what we've had for as long as I can remember. So this is what I propose to you, let's start over. I want us to be able to talk to each other and treat one another with the respect that each of us deserve. Siblings fight from time to time, but I think we've both matured to the point where we can be friends, if you're willing to give it a shot.

Moira, it may not seem like it but I love you so, so much, and I'm more proud of you than you can ever know. Whether it's you sending me a text telling me you aced your junior paper, or seeing you at the State cheerleading competition in front of thousands of people, I may not come out and say it but I'm always thinking, "Wow, that's my little sister." I don't like admitting it but you're so much better than me at a lot of things like school, managing money, having a great work ethic. All these things make me feel lucky to call myself your brother. I know I've always been a little over-protective of you when it comes to guys but it's only because I only want you to be with a guy that truly deserves you and really appreciates you for the amazing young woman you are.

I guess just to wrap up this novel of a letter, cherish this weekend and realize all you can get out of it as long as you give as much as you can. I can't wait to give you the biggest hug in the world when you get home. I'm so excited to see what this weekend does for you. I love you will all of my heart, Moira, and even though I can be a pain in the ass and seem like I don't care, just know that no matter what, we're family and you can always count on me.

With tons of love,
Your older, protective brother, Conner

P.S.   I bet my letter totally made you cry?! :-P

chapter sixteen
gratitude

I see him sometimes at the oddest places and the oddest times and for only the briefest of moments. I may be crossing a parking lot and out of the corner of my eye, I'll see him. Or maybe it is while shopping at the mall or just walking downtown. It's not him, of course, but for just a flash—for just a fraction of a second—time freezes, I feel my heart lighten and a smile start to come to my lips. I get that all-too-brief feeling in my heart that it really is him but then I look closer and realize it isn't.

Maybe it was the color or cut of his hair or the way he was dressed or, perhaps, even just the way he was standing, that reminded me of him. That brief feeling of elation is replaced with a deep, but momentary, sadness and then a realization that if that is all I get to see of Conner that day, that will have to be enough. That brief flicker of memory means he is still alive, at least to me.

-Jane Luby

Perhaps what allows me to retain at least a shred of sanity is my innate optimism. I always seem to find the best side of almost every situation. I generally don't allow myself to accept defeat. The sun will always rise tomorrow. Failure is not always final. Success is right around the corner. These have never been just platitudes to me. This is really how I function and this is what allows me to stave off the darkness, at least most of the time.

In the weeks and months following Conner's death, this attitude proved a lifesaver for both Jane and me because it allowed us to seek, and eventually find, some good out of our loss. This attitude allowed us to appreciate what we had rather than dwelling on what we had lost. This attitude gave us the ability to appreciate who Moira was becoming, and her accomplishments, rather than losing ourselves in the grief surrounding Conner's death.

In moments of reflection—and there were many of those—I thought about how I would not be able to observe Conner becoming a man, a husband, and a father. I wouldn't be able to teach him how to replace a sash cord in a double-hung window as my dad had done for me. I would never be able to teach him how to build a bookshelf or help him put together IKEA furniture. I wouldn't be able to help him overcome the obstacles and mistakes that everyone experiences throughout their lives. I would think about all of the pearls of wisdom I had learned over the years and that had been handed down to me by my father and others whom I respected. I would never be able share these pearls with my son. I was determined to be a better father than my own was and looked forward to continuing to teach and counsel Conner so that he could someday become a better father than me.

While these sad thoughts certainly arose from time to time, I tried my best to subvert them, to cage them, and only allow them to surface in moments of weakness. They arose during those times when, whether voluntarily or not, I went dark. Otherwise, I tried to recognize how I would still experience many of these same joys with Moira and that would be enough; it would have to be enough. This is not intended to be a slight to Moira. Rather, it is to recognize that I always envisioned my future involving both of my children, watching both of my children mature and enter the real world, and enjoying them both as they married and raised their families. Now, there was just one child. No matter how wonderful Moira is—and she truly is wonderful—she is still only one-half of the pair.

Jane and I learned to cope by focusing on the fact that we had nearly twenty-one years of mostly wonderful memories of Conner, rather then dwelling on a future that had so suddenly evaporated. We came to view Conner's death as what had been avoided rather than what had been lost. The fact is, at the time of the accident, Conner was alone in the car. He was coming back from a party where he'd spent time with friends. He could just as easily have had these friends with him in the car when he ran into the back of the asphalt carrier. In fact, he had invited a friend, Jeff Polits, to join him that evening. Jeff, however, had been working and declined the offer due to fatigue. Had he gone along with Conner, we might have lost him too.

Conner could just as easily have run into another car, thereby injuring or killing innocent people, rather than crashing into a multi-ton truck. We were able to appreciate, and be grateful for, the fact that only a single life was lost and that ours was the only family directly devastated.

We learned to become grateful that Conner died instantly from the impact. The Saab struck the asphalt carrier with such force that the rear end of the car actually crumpled up, bent over the front and also struck the carrier. We considered ourselves fortunate that he didn't suffer; he didn't feel the impact. We subsequently found out that the brakes hadn't been touched, which indicated that he hadn't even seen the truck. Whether he had passed out, fallen asleep, or merely been distracted, he did not see his impending death. He didn't experience the horror, no matter how momentary, of knowing what was coming.

He didn't feel the car tumble and flip upside down immediately after the impact. He didn't feel the flames that subsequently engulfed the car and, of course, his body.

Perhaps most unimaginable to many is how we consider ourselves fortunate that Conner died rather than somehow surviving to live on, horribly disfigured or disabled. I know this sounds shallow and may be offensive to some. I know this might make us sound like awful parents. I know this sentiment requires us to prefer losing our son entirely rather than just losing some of his superficial physical abilities. To understand this, however, you need to have known and understood Conner.

In the last stages of my father's battle with cancer, he chose to continue to fight, without regard for quality of life, because of his fear of death. Whether because of a lack of faith or a fear of final judgment and retribution, he dreaded his final passing. He fought it even though he had to give up all the things that had previously made life worth living for him. It was a painful battle to watch, especially as we all knew it was one that could not be won.

Unlike my father, I have no fear of my death and never have. I certainly fear pain; I fear being unable to do things that bring me happiness; and I fear the distress that my death will cause my wife and daughter. I do not, however, have any fear of my own demise. It's not a matter of religious faith, as I truly have no idea of what, if anything, happens next. I take comfort in completely rejecting the notion that I will be punished for not accepting any particular deity as my lord and savior. I take comfort in rejecting the notion of some all-knowing deity judging me for my actions, words, and/or thoughts.

I prefer to look at death as an adventure, a leap into the unknown. Either it's "lights out" and nothing is there or, alternatively, there is some continuation of our existence. If it's "lights out," then there will be no regret. If there is some continuation of existence, then it is an opportunity to experience something new and exciting. Either way, fear is not involved, and instead, I am curious. Perhaps most importantly, I hold on to the hope of being able to reconnect with loved ones lost and, in particular, with Conner.

So this brings us back to why we believe that it might be better that Conner died rather than surviving the accident. The problem is that to focus on what *we* want is selfish. Of course, I would love to talk to Conner again. I would love to hold him, to comfort him – even if only for a moment. I would give almost anything to be able to tell him how wonderful he is and how much I love him. The question, though, is whether that would be fair to him? The question that needs to be asked is whether Conner would have wanted to survive like that.

We, as his family and friends, need to look at how, and whether, Conner could have dealt with severe disfigurement, paralysis, and/or some other type of debilitating condition. We need to consider whether Conner would have preferred a quick death to a lingering life of anger and regret.

Conner was a lot of things. He was loving and joyful, but he was also vain and proud. He was a free spirit, but at some point, we all knew that he was going to have to grow up, accept responsibility, and gain control of his tendencies to fly off in a million different directions at once. While I believe that he was capable of great things, I don't believe that he had the emotional strength to accept debilitating physical changes that would have prohibited him from living the type of life he always sought. At twenty years of age, he simply didn't have the emotional fortitude and maturity to withstand such challenges. I fear that we would have seen that spark in Conner's eye gradually diminish and ultimately flicker out, to be replaced with something else. I fear that we would have seen Conner's effervescence and love of life consumed by bitterness and anger. I believe that we would have seen his innate joy poisoned by regret and self-pity; that he would lose all semblance of being "Conner." Without his innate joyfulness, that pervasive attribute that made him so loved and memorable to so many, he would not have been Conner. And he would have hated that.

Many people are able to live amazing lives by overcoming daunting obstacles and handicaps. I admire these people; they are truly remarkable. They choose to persevere rather than to give up. They choose to accept their physical challenges in order to help themselves and others. These people are courageous and wonderful—I just don't think that my son could have been one of them. Of course, I'm not sure that I could be one of them either.

It takes an incredible amount of internal strength to be able to overcome drastic change in one's physical abilities. Over my life, my body has failed in various ways but they have always been relatively minor failures. I used to be a runner but, after surgery for a torn meniscus, the surgeon discovered that the result of a lack of cartilage in my left knee was bone-on-bone contact. My running days were over. I was able to adapt, however, and engage in other activities. I rode bikes; I hiked and climbed mountains; I engaged in adventure races; I took up soccer, and squash, and played golf. I adapted my physical activities to the gradual physical deterioration of my body.

These physical changes, however, are insignificant as they are little more than the natural and gradual deterioration of the human body and reminders of the aging process. Even when I was diagnosed with leukemia, I knew that it would be a gradual disease and that I would be able to adapt as the symptoms progressed.

I have a good friend with multiple sclerosis. Ken Cruickshank has been immensely successful in both his career and personal life. I have watched over the years as his disease robbed him, first of his career and then of his mobility. I have watched him regress from walking with a cane to a wheelchair. I have watched his physical strength and independence ebb and have seen how he sharpened his mind to compensate for the failure of his body so as to maintain a quality of life that was acceptable to him. I have marveled over his emotional strength to be able to handle the progression of this terrible disease with remarkable grace and courage.

My sister Maureen has a more slowly progressive form of MS. Nonetheless, I have watched her also lose her mobility and have seen how it has affected her ability to engage in ordinary and everyday activities. I have seen her anger and frustration as her body slowly and methodically betrays her. I have seen the effect this disease has had on her life and personality as the slope keeps getting more and more steep and slippery and she slides downhill at an increasingly more rapid pace.

I question whether I would be able to exhibit the same strength, grace, and courage as Ken and Maureen, and have a strong suspicion that the answer would be no. I don't question, but truly and completely believe in my heart, that Conner would not have been strong enough either. Perhaps one day he might have had that type of strength and courage, but not at twenty years of age. I'm grateful that he didn't have to experience those challenges and experience those frustrations.

Selfishly, perhaps, I'm grateful for the memories of my son as he was, rather than as the bitter and angry person he might have turned into. My mother was always a sweet person, a mother who did her best with sometimes difficult situations. In the last years of her life, as the senility took hold, she turned into a bitter and angry woman. She could be violent; she would utter racial slurs; she changed into someone other than the woman who had raised me. This was not how I wanted to remember my mother and this remains a source of anger. I could accept her passing but I hated the way she passed.

Similarly, if Conner had somehow survived but been consumed by bitterness and anger, what would that have done to all of us? At the moment of his death, we were all in a good place. We were all happy and were getting along as well as any family can. I look back and have wonderful memories and feelings about him because at the time he passed, there were no issues of anger or jealousy or disappointment. In those early morning hours of September 12, 2009, before he stepped into that car, Conner was perfect and that, more than anything else, is how I choose to remember him.

chapter seventeen
the one

Conner always treated me with such respect, the kind of respect that I see my Dad give to my Mom. He always put me first. There was a night when I was staying at his house and I was getting really sick with a chest cold. I couldn't stop coughing. Conner got up in the middle of the night and drove to Walgreens and got what seemed like every type of cold medicine possible. He came back and I still couldn't sleep because of the coughing. He gave me this medicine and just stayed with me, braiding my hair and making sure I drank a lot of water.

I'd never been in the type of relationship before where someone put the other person before himself. He did this truly and genuinely without the thought of getting anything in return. He taught me how to be in a relationship - a real relationship. He taught me how to be a partner and how to respect my partner. I will always be grateful to him for teaching me that.

I don't know if you remember the Father's Day card that I sent you that summer – the summer that Conner and I dated. I just wanted to thank you for raising such a wonderful son. I'd never written anything like that before…or since.

-Danielle Winterhalter

While he was a wonderful friend, especially to those in need, he could be annoying, mostly because he loved to argue. He was highly opinionated but not in the same way as so many of his peers. He held strong opinions but was smart enough to know he could be wrong. Conner understood that he wasn't always the smartest person in the room, and he would listen to others' points of view and learn from them. He gave his opinions without concern for political correctness and often without tact. He could be crass and he could be outrageous in his opinions.

Conner just loved to talk and sometimes this love of talk turned into debate. Unless you held a belief he thought was hateful—i.e., racism, sexism, violence, etc.—he would listen to your opinion and absorb what he found credible and reject what just didn't make sense to him. He and I had numerous debates throughout his childhood, and I often took the opposite side of the debate, regardless of my personal beliefs, just to show him that there were usually at least two sides to every issue. He understood what I was doing in playing the devil's advocate but still relished the opportunity to challenge, and occasionally to best me in debate.

He learned a lot by argument and debate and would talk to anyone and argue about anything in order to increase his knowledge. Learning by debate was always more fun and natural than merely reading. I recall receiving a call from him one evening. He proceeded to excitedly tell me how he had just completed a debate with a Jesuit priest named Father Rick Ganz. He told me that they had been debating some esoteric religious issue and that he had won the argument when the priest finally capitulated. Now I don't know if Fr. Ganz gave up because Conner had actually won the day or from the sheer exhaustion of arguing with an inexhaustibly energetic teenage boy. In either event, Conner interpreted this as a vindication of his intellect and logic and took great joy in that.

He used his gift of gab to talk to anyone and everyone. Most often, he seemed to use it to charm peers and adults, teachers and coworkers. He found the way to ingratiate himself to others. His charm was particularly effective when directed at the opposite sex, regardless of age. Mothers and grandmothers found him to be sweet and flirtatious in an innocent, yet flattering, way. For those of you of a sufficient age, you may remember Eddie Haskell from the television show *Leave It To Beaver*. That was Conner. He always complimented the older women—on their hair, their clothes, or their wit. It wasn't a sexual thing but, rather, a type of innocent flattery that made him so memorable. He enjoyed flattering women and making them feel good about themselves, and they enjoyed the attention of a handsome young man.

He forever established his primacy amongst the grandchildren by doing something as simple as bringing an inexpensive bouquet of flowers to his grandmother. As long as she was coherent, she always broke into a smile when Conner's name came up in a conversation, and she would always talk about the flowers that he brought her.

For the girls his age, however, his charm had a much less innocent purpose. We were never a particularly religious family and I was determined not to saddle either of our kids with the Catholic guilt about sex that had been hammered into me for more years than I care to remember. We, as a family, were very open about sex. We talked about it, and joked about it, all without the burden of shame. Conner and Moira knew their parents were sexually active, although we did our best to shield them from anything more than innocent displays of affection.

* * *

Before Jane and I met, I dated a lot of girls but never for longer than two months. I would become attracted to a girl and then, when the attraction was reciprocal, became infatuated. Eventually, however, I would find some flaw or deficiency in the girl and the infatuation would end quicker than it began. Once I knew that a girl wasn't "The One," I moved on. In hindsight, some of these flaws and deficiencies were ridiculously petty, but I knew what I was looking for and I wouldn't settle for anything less. She didn't need to be perfect; she just needed to be perfect for me.

This may have been unfair to some of the girls that I dated, but I always knew that there was one particular person out there for me, that one person with whom I could build a life and a family. Wasting time with someone who wasn't that person didn't seem fair to either them or me. More importantly, I didn't want to take a chance on missing "The One" by being involved with someone else. That obviously all changed when I met Jane.

After two months with Jane, I was still head over heals in love. After six months, I was even more in love with her. After nine months, I knew she was The One and proposed shortly thereafter. I suspect that Conner's serial relationships were all part of his search for his "Jane." He appreciated the relationship that his parents had and he wanted one of his own. It may not have been Sami or Emily or Danielle, it may not have been any of the other girls he dated, but The One was out there and he knew it. With every relationship, he matured a little bit more and began to better understand what he needed and what he needed to become.

Like any married couple, Jane and I fought and sometimes Conner and Moira would see us doing so. As neither of us is particularly adept at hiding anger, the children knew if we had been fighting, even if they hadn't witnessed the actual argument. While we generally kept our more heated conversations behind closed doors, we also knew that it was important for the children to see us argue. They needed to know that even happily married couples argue and that a simple argument did not change the love that Jane and I felt for one another. It was important for both kids to understood that arguments come with relationships, and that people are just not always happy with one another all of the time. We used to tell the kids when we were particularly angry with them that we might not like them right then and there but we still loved them.

More commonly, they saw us deal with the complexities of modern life. They saw us communicate and relate to one another and them, sometimes with humor, other times with anger, but always with a deep and abiding respect.

One of our oldest family traditions is that Jane and I kiss before every meal, whether at home, with friends, or in a restaurant. I'm not sure when this started but I know we always wanted our children to see and understand true affection. On those few occasions when Jane and

I might be distracted and forget to kiss before a meal, one or both of the kids would always remind us. This is something they watched for. In an age where divorce is so rampant, this was a reassurance to them that Jane and I were solid. It was a reaffirmation of our love and commitment to one another. It is a tradition that we continue even with our empty nest, now more of a reassurance to each other than to anyone else.

* * *

Over the years, especially with the arrival of puberty, Conner dated a lot of girls. What was interesting, at least to us as his parents, is how quickly we learned whether a girl was truly special to him. It was very common for him to have friends at the house, both guys and girls. We didn't always know if there was a romantic connection with the girls. Some of the girls were clearly "buds." They were girls with whom he built and maintained strong and lasting friendships, relationships uncluttered with the complexities of sexual politics. Other girls were friends he had met and we didn't know whether they were just a momentary acquaintance or something more.

We did note, however, that it was very rare for him to introduce a girl to us unless he had special feelings toward her, either as a "bud" or as a true girlfriend. If Conner invited a girl to dinner, we knew that he had special feelings about her. If we just met a girl in passing, we generally referred to her as the "flavor of the week." Sometimes those weeks only lasted days, or even just hours, and we might never see the girl again.

There were only a handful of real girlfriends that we truly got to know over the years – primarily Sami, Emily, Fallon, and Danielle. These girls ran the gamut as far as modesty, intellect, and personality but the traits they shared were that they were all genuinely good people. Of course, they were also attractive but that is beside the point, and we expected nothing less. These few girls were the type of girls Conner not only wanted to bring home to meet his parents, but with whom he was proud to be seen. It wasn't just about sex with them and we're still not sure to what level these varied relationships went. It was about building and maintaining a deeply personal and lasting bond. It was about learning to respect and care for someone else. It was about developing the type of lasting and healthy relationship that he observed in his parents' relationship. These girlfriends, and there were only a very few of them, made him a better person and he knew it.

chapter eighteen
do-overs

I remember one instance when he called me up asking if I wanted to go to a basketball game at some random school about 20 miles away. I said sure as I always did. My network was about the size of a pea compared to his vegetable garden of friends.

When we got there, he told me he wanted to see his friend Mike play; there wasn't anyone else he was there to meet. Sure enough, 20 minutes later, he has a posse of about 10 people all hanging around him, girls and guys, saying how much they missed him and how they've been meaning to call him and so on and so forth. The most amazing part was that he remembered all their names while I struggle half the time to remember the names of my closest friends. That was just the kind of guy he was.

-Jonathon Pelzner

In hindsight, I know there are many things I would do differently if given the opportunity. Perhaps I would have been tougher on Conner and done a better job of instilling discipline. Perhaps I would have put greater emphasis on the importance of studying and grades. Perhaps I would have spent more time with him instead of working so much and pursuing my own recreational activities and hobbies. Of course, had I done so, I might have altered who Conner was and what he meant to others. Change is always a difficult concept and not all change is for the best.

I once heard a writer speaking about a study in which parents with children who had various disabilities were asked whether, if they could go back in time, they would "change" their kids so that they could be "normal." The nearly universal response was no. Certainly, these parents wished their children to be cured or to be able to lead a "normal" life, but the parents loved the children they had and loved them for who they were. They understood that any change in their circumstance could also change who the kids were. Their various disabilities had helped shape them into the people they were now, and to take away the disability might take away what made their child so special.

I take great pride in the man Conner was when he died but I take even greater pride in the man he was becoming. If I could go back in time, I would not change a single thing about him. For me, he really was perfect. That being said, I wasn't. I want a do-over. I want the chance to correct the mistakes I made. I want the chance to be a better father to him. I know in my heart that I was a good father and that Conner loved me. I know that he appreciated all I did for him…but I could have done more and I could have done it better. He deserved both more and better.

There are four specific instances that stick with me and drive my feelings of failure. I recognize that these are small matters and may be little more than my own personal conceit, but they stick with me. The first was when Conner was only one year old. It was the Saturday of the Notre Dame v. USC football game. Jane was out and I was watching the game on television with Conner in my lap. It was a close game and Conner was fussing. He kept crying and nothing I did could ease his discomfort. The more he cried, the more it interfered with my watching of the game and the angrier I got.

Finally, I put him in the car and took him to the doctor. I remember muttering under my breath as we drove that he really better have something really wrong or else. I was pissed about missing the game. We got to the doctor's office and after a quick examination, he was diagnosed with a double ear infection. I can't explain the guilt I felt. I felt complete and abject shame. I wish I could say that that was the last time I put my interests before those of my son, but I can't. While it had no long-lasting effect upon Conner, either physically or emotionally, it is one of those acts of immaturity and selfishness that I could never forget and that, with his death, only becomes clearer.

* * *

When Conner was in kindergarten, we signed him up for soccer. At that age it was appropriately called "Kick 'n Chase" and I volunteered to be a coach. I had never played soccer in my life and had only a very basic understanding of the game. Nonetheless, I was one of those bewildered fathers calling out conflicting instructions to the players.

The following year was Conner's first season of "real soccer." I volunteered to be the assistant coach and quickly figured out the basics of the game and what I didn't like about the head coach's personality and tactics. The following year, and thereafter, I was the head coach. My job as head coach was threefold: teach the fundamentals of the game; give the players some exercise; and make sure that they have fun. I was adequate at the first two duties and generally excelled at the third.

When Moira was in first grade, we signed her up for soccer and I decided that it was only fair that I start coaching her and let some other father coach Conner's teams. I well remember my rationale at the time—I didn't have time to coach two soccer teams. I was managing my own law practice and just couldn't handle more coaching duties. The truth, however, is that I could have done it. I could have coached both teams but I found a reason to excuse my laziness.

Certainly, we attended all of Conner's soccer games, and I continued coaching his basketball teams for another year or so, but the truth was that I really wish that I had continued to coach him. I'm not so egotistical to think that he would have become a better soccer player, or that if I had continued to coach he somehow wouldn't have died. Rather, had I made more of an effort, his much-too-short of a life might have been just a little better for him and, for me, I could have spent more time with him.

* * *

In middle school, Conner took a class on drug abuse. At that time, he was very impressionable and vehemently opposed to drugs. One night he asked me if I had ever taken drugs. I said yes.

He looked at me with that look he used to give me when I was trying to trick him, and said, "No, I don't mean prescription drugs, I mean illegal drugs like pot."

I again said yes. He looked crestfallen. I tried to explain to him that when I was in college, I tried pot but that I didn't like it and stopped using it. This wasn't entirely truthful, but I felt some compulsion to show him that I made mistakes too. Later that night I walked by his room and he had posted a piece of paper on his bedroom door that said, "No Druggies!" When I knocked on his door, he told me to go away.

I feel guilty about that. I thought that I was being progressive by being substantially honest with my seventh-grade son. What I hadn't considered was how it would make him feel. He had just attended a program that talked about the dangers of illegal drugs, and then he found out that his own father had abused drugs. While he seemed fine by the time we had breakfast in the morning, I understood that I had put my own political beliefs as to the Drug War before the feelings and best interests of my son. I should have taken into account his age and waited until he was just a bit older before starting to let him know of my failures and inadequacies. He wanted his father to be this larger-than-life figure; perhaps he needed me to be that figure, and I failed him. A better father would have handled it differently.

* * *

Finally, I feel guilty about not encouraging Conner to pursue his interest in music. He had a great voice and a passion for music, but it never occurred to me to encourage him take singing lessons. One year he asked for an electric guitar for his birthday. Rather than just agreeing and buying him an inexpensive guitar, I told him that he could use my acoustic guitar and that if he stuck with it, we would eventually buy him an electric guitar. What was the purpose of that? His interest was in rock music, not in acoustic music. If only I had only purchased him an electric guitar, perhaps he would have loved it and explored new opportunities. Perhaps he would have been happier and more successful. It wasn't the cost of an electric guitar that stopped me but, rather, my own stubbornness. I wanted to teach him a lesson about "earning" the right to pursue an interest. As I had on countless other occasions, I put my need to teach him an insignificant lesson ahead of my duty as a parent to encourage him to explore and pursue his interests. I was an ass and I feel guilty about that.

While I don't blame myself directly for the accident, I still think back over the nearly twenty-one years of his life and see my failures as a father more than my successes. I have to wonder whether, if I had done something differently over the course of his life, if I had been a better father, was it possible that Conner might have made different decisions on the evening of September 11 and the early morning hours of September 12? I wonder if somehow the cumulative effect of my parenting inadequacies and mistakes had contributed to his death.

* * *

Regardless of how many times that Jane and Moira reassure me that I was, and am, a wonderful father, I know the truth. I could have been better. I should have been better. Of course, had I done so, I might have altered who Conner was and what he meant to others. That sentiment is, however, merely a rationalization that I use to assuage my guilty conscience. I want to go back and do things differently. I want to go back and appreciate what I had. I want to go back and be a better father. I want a do-over.

chapter nineteen
the wrath of moira

Jane mentioned to me once about Conner's energy and how much she missed it. I didn't know Conner personally but we had a daughter in his class and another daughter in Moira's class. We became friends with Kevin and Jane only after Conner's death. I was fascinated to hear so much about this obviously special boy who exuded this special energy. I felt like I got to know him, at least a little bit.

One evening after dinner with Kevin and Jane, I had a visit from Conner. I don't consider it to be a dream because it was so very different than a dream. In any event, Conner appeared and said to me, "So, you want to see my energy, huh?" Immediately and before I could even answer, I saw the most magnificent display of swirling, racing, and flashing colors. As an artist I was stunned by the display. It was like nothing I had ever seen before or since.

-Karen Cruickshank

I somehow knew, almost immediately after the call from Moira, that we were going to need some sort of grief counseling. I knew Jane wasn't emotionally strong enough to weather this disaster without professional help. I knew this would completely change who Moira was and, without counseling, I was concerned that it might eventually destroy the both of them and, in effect, destroy the "us" that remained. It is one thing to have your childhood destroyed by an event like this, but to have it destroy the rest of her life was more than I could accept. For myself, I knew that counseling might help me but, quite frankly, that was neither my concern nor focus.

I called around and found that most grief counselors had a waiting list. Fortunately, I was friendly with a clinical psychologist, Linda Nishi-Strattner, and she agreed to meet with us. While we only saw her sporadically over the six or seven months following Conner's accident, she was of immense help. From these sessions, two things really stand out.

She told us that the first year was not, in fact, going to be the toughest year. She explained that this was a common misperception. Certainly, Conner's twenty-first birthday, Moira's seventeenth birthday, Jane's birthday, my birthday, our first Thanksgiving, our first Christmas – all of those events were going to be difficult but they wouldn't be the toughest. She told us that during the first year, our friends and family would make a special effort to be with us and to help fill the void caused by Conner's absence. This they certainly did and we found great comfort in them.

It would be, however, the second year when those same friends and family members started falling by the wayside. They would go back to their normal lives and we would begin to experience what the rest of our lives would be like. That is when we would discover what our lives would be like without the distraction and camaraderie of friends and family. Year two is when we would find out what life without Conner was really going to be like and it would be terrible.

I am incredibly grateful that Linda warned us of this. She was absolutely correct and, as a result, we were able to prepare for and adjust to this new reality. I remember sitting with Jane and Moira on our second Christmas after Conner's death. It was quiet and calm. It was so unlike the bedlam and mayhem that we had been used to. When Conner was alive, groups of friends were always coming and going. The first Christmas after Conner died, friends and family visited and made the effort to spend time with us. The second Christmas, however, was much more solitary. We all sensed that this was the new normal; this was our new life. Interspersed amongst the excitement of opening gifts and general holiday cheer came bouts of depression and tears. The silence that would normally have been shattered by Conner remained unbroken and relentless.

Jane, in particular, had difficulty recognizing the joy of the holiday season. She, perhaps more than Moira or me, recognized the void that was all-too-often present. Nonetheless, Jane recognized that it wasn't fair to Moira to have her also lose the joy and cheer surrounding Christmas. As such, we maintained most of our traditions and still hung Conner's stocking from the fireplace mantel. We still managed to purchase and wrap gifts in tinfoil for one another to remind us that Conner would have gotten us presents if he were still alive. We still had our traditional eggs benedict and lobster chowder. We still celebrated, even if the celebration was forced.

The second thing of note from the grief counseling was the biggest surprise. Linda gave us a little quiz one day. This was about three or four months into our counseling and she asked us to take a short quiz that dealt with how each of us thought we were dealing with Conner's death. The questions involved matters like altered sleep patterns, bouts of sadness, and feelings of anger. Afterward, she asked us who we thought was having the toughest time in dealing with the loss. We all agreed that it was Jane. Even Jane thought so. After all, she and Conner were so much alike and, quite frankly, she wasn't as emotionally tough as Moira and me. Jane lost her father when she was only twenty-one years old and she had taken his death very badly. Conner's death brought back all of that pain and so much more.

Linda reviewed the quiz results and told us that, in fact, it was Moira who was having the toughest time. I was shocked. I had been fooled by her tough façade but had forgotten that Moira was only sixteen years old when she answered the door that September morning. She buried much of her pain and anger and managed to fool me. While she erupted from time to time, she generally seemed to be handling Conner's death at least as well as I was. Now we knew that this was just a charade, a mask similar to the one that I wore so often. Now we knew that Moira was where our focus needed to be.

After that time, Jane and I really started to notice the manifestations of Moira's grief. The pain seeped out through the cracks and usually in the form of anger. She was quick to get angry and displayed little patience with either friends or family. Jane was often the victim of her anger but her friends were also subjected to what we came to call "The Wrath of Moira." While this became frustrating for us, the impact upon her friends was greater. Her anger and impatience had the effect of pushing her friends away. While our love was unconditional and we could weather the storms that brewed within her, most of her friends had neither the ability nor the inclination to do so and, as a result, Moira became more isolated.

Fortunately for her, she met Roger Boulden a few months after Conner died. They began a long, and sometimes tumultuous, relationship as Roger became her first true love. We will always be grateful to Roger for helping to rescue Moira from the pit of despair and to help her salvage at least a portion of her childhood from the wreckage of Conner's accident.

chapter twenty

signs

I was working with a Shamanic healer one day when Conner came to us. We both kept feeling a presence coming in. The healer said, "There's this light that keeps coming in. Someone really wants something."

I asked, "Is it Conner?"

She paused for a moment and then said, "Yeah, it's Conner."

I asked what he had to say and then, all of a sudden, I could feel him talking to me. It wasn't words but I could sense him talking to me. He told me "Tell my parents that I am okay; that I am safe. Tell them that I am still with them and that I love them. Tell Moira that I love her too."

I did.

-Louise Botterill

Neither Jane nor I are religious. In fact, over the years I have shaken off my nearly fifteen years of Catholic education and fully embraced atheism and, on occasion, that atheism becomes strident. This is not to suggest that I never contemplate what happens after we shed our mortal coil. This concept was, however, always a matter of curiosity rather than any sort of burning need to explain how we came to be and where we go. I never felt a need to rely upon any particular explanation as to what happens before we are born and after we die. I am comfortable with my ignorance.

I had read extensively on various religions, primarily Judaism, Christianity, Islam, and Mormonism, but considered them to be little more than fascinating mythologies, akin to the wonderful Roman and Greek mythologies. All of these mythologies teach a moral code that can be, and generally is, admirable although they also, all too often, provide a justification for unimaginable deeds of sadism and hatred.

I should note that many years ago I read a book called *Becoming A Jew* on the off chance that I might want to convert to Judaism. Judaism is the foundation of most modern religions and carries a certain degree of respectability and spirituality. There were two reasons that I decided against becoming a Jewish convert. First of all, I found out that I would not be able to eat lobster as that was not considered to be kosher. I love lobster. The second reason, and in hindsight the true deal killer, was that you had to believe in a god. That seemed to be a constant in all of these religions, not just Judaism, and became the one obstacle that I couldn't overcome. I just could not find a way to blindly accept the possibility that there was some all-knowing and all-powerful paternal figure that loved us but allowed us to commit so many grotesque acts of violence to and upon one another. I remain spiritual and curious but not religious.

With Conner's death, I began to spend more time thinking about the possibility of a hereafter. For reasons that may be part delusional, I began to believe that death is not the end but, rather, that we somehow continue a form of existence, perhaps in other dimensions or planes of existence. I found comfort in the thought that Conner might still be alive somewhere. I found comfort in the thought that I might see him again one day.

* * *

Immediately after Conner's death, we began to experience unusual happenings. Light bulbs burned out significantly more often than they did when he was still alive. We discovered coins in odd places, such as in a pocket of a coat or the pages of a magazine. They might show up on a countertop or under the sheets of a bed that had just been made up that morning. Without obvious explanation, this reminded us of the old poem *Pennies From Heaven*.

During Conner's Irish Wake, Jane was talking to our niece Lindsay and Lindsay put her glass on the breakfast bar. Suddenly, the glass slid about eighteen inches and fell onto the floor. We were all startled and examined the counter surface. There was no moisture or anything else that would explain the movement of the glass.

One day in early October 2009, Jane pointed out that an open cupboard door in the kitchen was noticeably vibrating. I went over and the door was clearly vibrating despite the fact that nothing else nearby was. A glass of water on the counter just below the cupboard door showed no evidence of any vibration. The door kept vibrating for the better part of a minute and then just suddenly stopped.

When Jane is driving in her car and wants to call me, she uses her Bluetooth connection and says "Call Kevin." About every four months or so, the telephone responds with "Calling Conner."

Other unusual occurrences involved odors. Jane has always had a highly developed sense of smell. She would often sense an odor that none of the rest of us could. Sometimes she smelled fresh fish that, to her, meant her father was near. When she was a young girl, her father used to take her fishing and the odor of fresh fish became the signature scent for him.

Just a few days after the accident, Jane was out to lunch with a group of family and she mentioned that she smelled fish. This wasn't cooked fish but, rather, like the odor of freshly gutted fish. Our niece Lindsay could smell it also but, curiously enough, they were the only two that could. There were ten other people there and none of them could smell it. As soon as Jane realized that it was her father's signature scent, the scent disappeared. She found great comfort in the thought that her father, dead for over twenty-five years, might have come back to comfort her.

Others in Jane's life also had signature scents. For her mother, it was pot roast and for her grandfather, it was pipe smoke. She smelled these odors at different times and places and for no obvious reason.

On the Sunday after the accident, Jane was up in Conner's room with her sister and a couple of friends. All of a sudden they all began noticing a variety of intermittent odors. First there was her mother's pot roast. Everyone could smell it. Then it changed to the fresh fish smell again. As soon as someone commented on the smell, it changed again, this time to the odor of pipe tobacco. Shortly after that, they smelled freshly-baked brownies, one of Conner's favorite desserts, and this became his signature scent. It appeared sporadically over the following years and always provided Jane with great comfort.

I have no rational explanation for most of these occurrences and I began to consider the possibility that Conner might still be around, although in some form that we could not easily recognize nor fully appreciate. I wondered where he was and, more importantly, how he was. The fact that he was dead did not mean that he was no longer my son. The fact that he was dead did not mean that I did not continue to worry about him. In a way, I actually worried about him even more then. When he was alive, there was always the chance that I would be able to help him and, notwithstanding the obvious irony, keep him safe. While he was alive, I could call him to make sure he was all right. Wherever he was now, I could do nothing for him. I couldn't check in on him. I felt helpless and so I searched for answers.

I read various books on spirituality and near-death experiences. Unfortunately, they were of little, if any, comfort. Some books purported to explain *exactly* what happens to our souls after we die. The problem, however, is that the authors invariably pose their opinions as fact. They *know* what happens to us after we die. Their certainty made me dismiss them as much as any priest or minister who claims to *know* what heaven and hell are like based solely upon what they have read and been taught.

The fact is that, at best, we may have opinions and beliefs as to whether there is a hereafter and, if so, what it is like. To the extent that anyone believes that they "know" what happens next, it is really just faith and all too often they confuse faith with fact. I bristle at those who refuse to be intellectually honest and acknowledge that there is a difference between fact and faith. Their faith, in the end, may end up being true but none of us can truly know that until we die and experience the truth of what comes next.

I began reading scientific articles and treatises about the possibility of multiple or quantum universes and interpenetrating dimensions. Is it possible that what we consider death involves just the four dimensions that we are aware of – length, width, depth and time? Is it possible that we continue to exist in additional dimensions? I began to develop my own personal concepts of what might happen after we die. It is a belief that is deeply personal and based solely and completely upon what I think and not what I know. All I know is that I *don't* know.

If it is possible that existence somehow continues, however, that might explain the existence of psychics. What if psychics are somehow able to sense one or more additional dimensions and to communicate with those that still exist there? Is it possible? I believe so.

Prior to the accident, I never truly believed in psychics and was more familiar with the charlatans and scam artists than with anyone that truly was able to speak with the dead. Nonetheless, I had to admit that some people certainly seemed to be able to glean information that only the dead and their close surviving loved ones might actually know. Perhaps they are just adept at reading people and telling them what they want to hear. Or, perhaps these psychics have an ability to experience other dimensions and communicate with those who remain in these other dimensions. At a minimum, it seemed to be a possibility.

Jane and her sister Laura have always believed in psychics. The day of Conner's death, Laura called her regular psychic Ann. This psychic, as a rule, does not take telephone calls on the weekend or otherwise do readings on her off days. This Saturday, however, she picked up the telephone. Laura told her that her nephew had just died but didn't give any details because she didn't know any of them. Ann told Laura that she could sense Conner. She explained how she saw him rolling down a grassy hill and, when he stood up, he was rubbing his head, unsure of where he was or what had happened. This was entirely consistent with the fact that Conner died immediately upon impact with severe head injuries. It was also consistent with the concept that, if somehow a part of Conner did survive, his death would have been so sudden and unexpected, that he would be confused.

In the coming months, Jane had a couple of telephone readings with this same psychic, as well as others. They seemed to be able to describe Conner's personality despite the fact that they never met him. They described his sense of humor, as well as his mischievousness. One psychic started laughing during a reading with Jane. She said that Conner was quite the jokester. When Jane asked her why she said that, the psychic explained that she always heard her "voices" in her left ear. That day, however, Conner insisted on speaking to her in her right ear.

Moira also—albeit somewhat reluctantly—went to a psychic about this time and found some comfort. This psychic told Moira that, at the time of the accident, Conner was looking down and reaching for something. She didn't know if it was his phone or a CD or something else but she was adamant that Conner was awake, but just distracted at the moment of the impact.

For Moira, however, the psychics and unusual occurrences were a mixed blessing. On the one hand, they suggested to her that her brother was still out there somewhere but, on the other hand, reminded her that he wasn't here. Further, the concept of giving credit to Conner for the inexplicable could be highly annoying.

For the first couple of years, Moira bristled any time that Jane would attribute some unexplained phenomenon to Conner. While Jane found comfort in giving Conner credit for the coins and burned out light bulbs, this angered Moira. When Jane talked of psychics, Moira would either erupt or storm off in a huff. She wasn't quite ready to forgive Conner for his mistake, and giving him credit for something he might have done on some metaphysical level seemed unfair and undeserved.

My amateur psychological assessment was that she was mad at Conner. She was mad at him for abandoning her. She was mad at him for making her an only child. She was mad at him for turning her into "the kid whose brother died." She was mad at him for causing so much pain to Jane and me.

While they bickered over the years as all siblings do, Moira enjoyed being Conner's little sister. She certainly didn't agree with all of his decisions, but she realized that his charisma and innate sense of joy were wonderful things to be around. She would never eclipse, or be eclipsed by, Conner because they were such different people. Nonetheless, she enjoyed basking in the reflected happiness that always seemed to surround him. She was proud to be Conner's little sister. Now that was gone and she was angry.

She had no obvious vent for her anger. She couldn't yell at him. She felt guilty about being mad at him because, at least in her mind, being mad at him was just wrong. He was dead and how can you be mad at someone who died? How do you make up with someone who is dead? How do you resolve unresolved disputes? This anger stayed with her for years.

Moira and I share many traits, both good and bad. In this case, she shared my disinclination to seek counseling to deal with the anger and grief. Instead she, like me, decided to take the lengthy and painful process of healing herself. This is not the easy way, and it certainly wasn't the way that Jane and I wanted her to handle it, but much like me, she needed to make her own decisions and her own mistakes.

Fortunately, and over time, Moira did forgive him. She too began to attribute seeming coincidences to Conner. She began to believe that psychics might be real. That was when we really knew that Moira was going to be okay, more because of the forgiveness than the psychics. As her anger ebbed, she blossomed.

* * *

In one of Jane's readings in the months after the accident, she was told that she would not experience any further heartache. The psychic seemed to understand how damaged Jane was, first by the death of her father and then, again, when Conner died. She assured Jane that she would never suffer like that again.

Jane found great comfort in this pronouncement and promptly told both Moira and me. We looked at one another, started to smile, and then said, "You understand, of course, that this just means that you are the next to go." Jane seemed startled at first by that revelation. While we laughed about this prediction, we understood that we all have to go sometime. If it would be easier on Jane that she goes next, so be it. Moira and I would soldier on somehow. While not inured to grief, even then we knew that we could survive it.

* * *

Over the last several years, all three of us have become fans of Theresa Caputo, the "Long Island Medium," whose show is on The Learning Channel. We enjoy her personality and her show certainly helps give credence to the possibility that mediums are real and that it is possible to speak with the departed. I can only hope that all of us, but particularly Jane and Moira, have an opportunity to "speak" with Conner again someday. I like to think that I would be open to hearing Conner speak through a medium but I'm not sure that I am, or that I ever will be. Something in me won't let me acknowledge that Conner might actually talk to me. Perhaps it is just my lack of faith or, maybe, it is something else. Perhaps I don't feel deserving of such a gift; maybe I need to learn how to forgive myself for my failures as a father before I can allow myself to consider the possibility of reconnecting with Conner. Perhaps it is because I am afraid of what Conner might say to me. Might this be akin to the fear that my father experienced before he died? He feared being judged by God; perhaps I fear being judged by Conner.

chapter twenty-one
a single red apple

I was a lowly freshman but, thanks to my cheerleading "family," I got the nerve to talk to the CUTEST sophomore boy to walk the halls of Jesuit High School. After a week or so, I invited him to come hang out on my family's boat. I'm pretty sure my heart jumped out of my throat when he said "well DUH. I'd love to hang out with a cute girl!"

As it happens, Saturday rolls around. I remember not even being able to sleep the night before as I was so excited. I got a text from him that morning telling me what time he'd be over. A few anxious hours later, Conner's name lit up on my phone. I answered expecting him to say he was outside, but he told me his car had run out of gas at few miles away.

I thought to myself, what a stupid excuse! He didn't have to make up some stupid story just to bail on me!

I quit getting ready and just sulked. An hour or so passed when I heard a knock at the door. Not wanting to do anything because - who wants to do anything with a broken heart, I let the poor person knock and knock. I finally dragged myself off of the couch and moped to the door. Looking out the window, I saw this mass of shaggy blonde hair. I timidly opened the door to see Conner standing there with a bouquet of flowers. He was sweating but had this amazing smile on his face.

"These are for you. I didn't have enough money to make a dent in my gas tank, so I bought these instead." He had walked all the way to my house because he had promised me he would come.

-Allie Hawes

It was just before our first Halloween when Moira told me that she was having a "Conner Day." She was feeling sad and couldn't stop thinking about what Halloween used to be like. While the children were growing up, we were always *that* house—the house with the skeletons and ghouls. Ours was the house that could sometimes be a bit too much for younger children. Ours was the house that generated the screams you could hear even in adjacent neighborhoods. Ours was the cool house.

One year, we created what appeared to be freshly dug graves in the front yard. The graves were actually made out of burlap and PVC pipe. Underneath we placed trash bags to give the impression of a mound. In the dark, they looked like freshly dug graves. I would hide under the burlap and when a parent bent over to inspect the "grave," I would jump up and terrify them.

Other years, Jane dressed up as Mother Bates, with fog drifting around the front door, or I dressed as a stuffed scarecrow to terrorize. Ours was the house you came to for entertainment more than for the candy.

That year, the first Halloween after Conner's death, we did nothing and that was what Moira was missing. This was why Moira was so sad that day. I explained to her that over the coming years, the emptiness that she was experiencing would be replaced by new memories and new traditions involving Halloween. Rather than decorating the house, we would go out to haunted houses. Rather than entertaining the neighborhood children and parents with our spooky house, we would scare Conner's friend Jeff Polits.

For reasons that I'm still not sure of, we developed a strong bond with Jeff immediately after Conner's death. We had known him a little in the past but we had always thought of him as just another of Conner's friends. After Conner's death, we discovered what a truly remarkable person he was. At first, it seemed that he needed us to help him through his grief, and we needed him as a reminder of the past. Over the following years, the need became a friendship and we began to admire him as a man. More than just about any of Conner's other friends, we found that Jeff shared many of the same innate traits with Conner including, unfortunately, a misplaced lack of confidence. We could see glimpses of the man Conner would have become in Jeff.

Back then, however, we were just starting to get to know Jeff. We learned that he hated clowns, especially scary clowns. That first Halloween, we hung a scary clown looking into a window beside Jeff's front door. When he came down the stairs, he would see a clown staring in at him.

The next year, Jeff was living with his father in a gated community. With Jane acting as lookout, I scaled the wall and hung a large scary clown from Jeff's car. Later that evening, when Jeff was taking the garbage cans out to the curb, he was startled to see that ghostly clown floating over his car.

The third year, Jeff was working at a pizza place. The store had closed and we could see Jeff, through the front window, doing the close-out on the cash register. We snuck up and hung a large scary clown on the front window. It was only a few seconds before Jeff saw it through his peripheral vision and jumped. Jane and I were hiding behind a car, watching the whole time. Silly and juvenile, I know, but this had become one of the new traditions that helped fill our void.

This tradition continued the following year and will continue as long as we are able. It is a tradition that Conner would have embraced.

* * *

Once we got through Halloween and all of our birthdays, the next big step was Thanksgiving and then Christmas. Jane's sister Laura invited us to join her and her family at their cabin just south of Buffalo for our first post-Conner Thanksgiving. We thought it would be a good idea to get out of town, to try something new, and to see if the distraction would do us good.

We flew into Cleveland and then off to Ellicottville, New York. The cabin was on the side of a hill, with a small pond, and was absolutely lovely. We settled in and, with forced smiles, began the Thanksgiving weekend.

David and Laura were wonderful hosts and their children, Lindsay and Drew, were great. Drew was only a few months older than Conner, and Lindsay was about five years older than her brother. A friend of Moira's, Jared, came down from Rochester Institute of Technology. Jared had been on Moira's Cheerleading Squad the prior year and Moira was the first person he had come out to. He brought a certain lightheartedness to the cabin and helped Moira laugh and smile throughout the weekend. He helped her forget, at least momentarily, who was missing that Thanksgiving.

I would get up early in the morning, put on my boots and cold weather gear, and head out to walk through the woods and explore. I had no destination in mind and never ran into another person. At one point, I found an apple tree covered in frost with only a single red apple remaining. I stared at the tree, trying to determine what cosmic message was being sent to me. Did the single red apple signify how Conner stood out from everyone else? Did it signify that life remained in me, despite my icy feelings of grief and despair? Or did it merely signify my desire to find some significance in an anomaly of nature?

I found a field, not too far from the cabin, and it became my safe place. I would lie down in the long, brown grass; listen to sad music; and gaze at the clouds floating overhead. While it was cold, being closer to the ground actually seemed to make it warmer. The ground had not yet frozen and by lying low in the grass, I was able to avoid most of the chilling wind. It was relaxing and allowed my mind to wander. I could think about Conner and what it meant now that he was gone. I could consider what the future might be like now that our family was down to just us three. I could process the prior two months, consider who I was becoming, and process what the future held for us. I discovered the beauty and expanse of simple contemplation.

One of the things I contemplated was how to go on, and even if I wanted to. Was it time to check out of the game? The life that I had constructed was now irretrievably gone. Was it even worth trying to rebuild from the ruins?

I need to state, first of all, that I am the kind of person who always thinks about possibilities and considers all options. Sometimes this involves looking at dark possibilities and options. Acknowledging that common parental fear, I had long considered the possibility of one of my children dying. Of course, this consideration had not prepared me for the reality of Conner's death. Nonetheless, it is my nature to look at possibilities and consider my options. One of those was suicide.

Years ago, a friend told me that she had attempted suicide when she was younger. When I inquired as to why, she explained that she felt as if she were caught in a downward spiral where she couldn't imagine a way out. For her, life would never get better; each day, each hour was worse than the one before. She couldn't fathom how the sun could ever shine again or how she could laugh again. Without any hope of escaping the all-encompassing despair, she decided to try and escape the darkness by overdosing.

My thought pattern wasn't like my friend's. While I was in pain, I didn't feel as if I was in an inescapable downward spiral. I *knew* that the sun would shine again; I *knew* that the day would come when I could laugh again. As such, my consideration was more objective, even clinical. I weighed the plusses and the minuses with a certain degree of detachment. I knew we had enough life insurance that neither Jane nor Moira would have any financial concerns. I also knew, however, that Jane and Moira needed me for much more than just financial reasons.

There was a television show back in the 1980s called *Thirtysomething*. It was an interesting, sometimes overly melodramatic, show that dealt with the lives and loves of a group of friends rapidly approaching middle age. While I remember little about the specifics of the show, one scene resonated and stayed with me to this day. In this particular scene, one of the characters, Nancy, was going through chemotherapy for breast cancer and was considering the uncertainty of her future. She and a friend, also going through chemotherapy, had gone out to the airport to drink wine and watch planes take off and land. They were sitting on the hood of a car, discussing the concept of mortality.

Nancy explained to her friend that she was unwilling to allow the cancer to win; she was unwilling to die, at least not at that point in her life. Her children were still young and they needed her. She was not done raising them yet, they needed their mother and she would not accept the possibility of succumbing to the cancer. Perhaps in a few years she could accept defeat but, right then and right there, she would be damned if she was going to let her children down.

That scene came to mind that morning. Moira was now seventeen years old but I was not done raising her. I still had so much left to do to help her develop into the woman she could become. She still needed me and I would be damned if I was going to let her down.

I also knew that if something were to happen to me, whether self-inflicted or otherwise, it would break both Jane and Moira. They had been through so much and were too fragile. Another emotional shock would be too much. I knew that I couldn't do that to them. I couldn't be responsible for the decimation of two lives.

In weighing the potential repercussions, it became quickly apparent that suicide was not an option. I felt no sense of relief in making this decision. This had been a clinical evaluation of an option. Once I determined that it wasn't a practical option, I forgot about it, never—at least to date—to consider it again.

In the cold, windy mornings out in my field, I continued my ruminations. What would life be like without Conner? How would we handle Christmas? We have always been a family steeped in traditions—some of them inherited, others created by us. We had the tradition of Jane and I kissing before every meal. We had a little song that we sang to one another in the weeks or days leading up to our birthdays. We had the goofy tradition of taking pictures on the first day of school, even if the children were away at college. The picture was always accompanied by a silly little song that was updated annually and, as last sung to Conner, went like this:

College Freshman Conner,
College Freshman Conner,
He's gonna save us all
And serve us ice cream and cake.

* * *

The Christmas season had, by far, the most traditions, three of which were particular favorites of mine.

The first tradition was that we, as a family, went out in early December of each year to select and cut down our Christmas tree. We would traipse through tree farms in neighboring counties, rain or shine. I will admit that this endeavor wasn't always as much fun as it might have been, but we always thought it important that the children be invested in the selection of our Christmas tree. Of course, the final arbiter of the choice was always Jane. The rest of us might make suggestions as to which tree to choose but the final decision was hers. The children and I would roll our eyes and mutter under our breaths from time to time as the selection process took much longer than we thought necessary. We knew, however, that Jane really did have the best "eye" for selecting the perfect tree. Further, we all knew that it was more important to Jane than to the rest of us.

Now the question was whether to go out tree hunting this year. Would all of the joy of the hunt for the perfect tree be extinguished by the overwhelming, and at times oppressive, absence of Conner? Would we be able to salvage this tradition and keep it as a bonding experience, or would we just end up just going through the motions, without any of the joy and excitement that that time of year usually brought?

Fortunately for us, Debra Henning, one of Jane's oldest and quirkiest friends, came out for a visit. It was a beautiful and cold December day and we found the perfect tree at only the second tree farm we stopped at. We were aware of the fact that Conner wasn't there with us but we kept the sadness at bay, hidden in the shadows cast by the bright sun. We managed to find our laughter and enjoyed the hunt. The tree was perfect and we knew that Conner would have approved. This would be a tradition to keep…at least until Moira moved away.

Another of my favorite holiday traditions was our annual Christmas card. As we have always had friends and family spread far and wide, and since this was before the emergence of the Internet and Facebook, we used picture Christmas cards as a way to stay in touch with people. This was our way of letting people see our family as it grew and evolved.

While some friends only sent pictures of their children, our pictures always included our entire family and always displayed our sometimes-peculiar sense of humor.

Jane and I started the tradition even before we were married. During my third year of law school, after we were engaged but well before we were married, Jane and I sent out our first Christmas card. For the photograph, Jane and I borrowed a classmate's infant, coincidentally named Connor. The picture showed the three of us, all dressed up in our holiday best. The greeting under the photograph was "Merry Christmas from the Lubys." We sent it out and more than a few people remarked to us, "I didn't realize that you and Jane were married." When we said that we weren't, we always enjoyed the look of confusion on the person's face.

The next year, our first as a married couple, our photograph was of Jane and me at Depoe Bay on the Oregon Coast. We were both holding a salmon in one hand and cradling a shotgun with the other. This, of course, led people to wonder what this had to do with Christmas; why we were fishing for salmon with shotguns; and, generally, what was wrong with us?

After Conner was born, our imaginations went wild. For our first Christmas as parents, Jane nixed my idea of having Conner lie on a platter in the middle of the dining room table, with the table set for a formal dinner. I pictured him lying on a bed of lettuce with, perhaps, an apple in his mouth. Jane thought this was in poor taste.

Another of my ideas, and one in keeping with the fishing theme from the prior year, was to have Jane and I holding Conner in a fishing net as if we had just caught ourselves a winner. This was also nixed by my lovely wife.

After much lighthearted debate, we finally agreed upon a picture. Our 1988 Christmas card photograph was of Conner in a basket outside our front door as Jane and I looked down, surprised to find an apparently abandoned infant on our doorstep.

With Moira's arrival, our options expanded. Having our picture taken on a fire truck with Moira dressed as a Dalmatian puppy seemed oddly appropriate. Having the four of us all dressed up, the girls in prom gowns, standing in front of a rusted truck, seemed apropos as well

Over the years and for truly unexplainable reasons, we began adding a red plastic fish, named "Gawky" by Conner, to our photographs. It actually became a bit of a challenge to friends and family to find Gawky in the photograph, similar to trying to find the bunny on the cover of *Playboy*. He might be peeking out from a napkin at a picnic or hidden in a tree behind us.

Our last picture with Conner was taken during a surprise snowstorm in December 2008. We hadn't yet decided on the theme of our photograph when the snow hit and shut down the area. We decided to head down to nearby Cook Park and found a beautiful setting with both trees and snow. We placed Gawky in the tree behind us and lined up with Jane and me in the middle, flanked by Conner and Moira. It was a beautiful picture of a very fortunate and good-looking family, perfectly capturing that moment in our lives. It is a picture that is never far from my thoughts, as it is one of the last pictures of our whole family.

The question we now contemplated was how, and whether, to continue with the family picture Christmas card tradition. If so, how would we handle the gaping void caused by Conner's death? My idea was to do a final Christmas card, this one with only Gawky pictured. To me, this was a way to close that chapter of our lives. For Jane, however, it was too much. We were not in a celebratory mood that Christmas and any Christmas card would be fake and insincere. After much discussion amongst the three of us, it was settled that this was a tradition to be retired.

Of course, Gawky has not been forgotten. He still comes out at Christmas time. We put him on a shelf, as another reminder of times gone by, and then he is put back in the closet until the following holiday season.

Our third principal Christmas tradition, and my personal favorite, involved creating a slideshow every year. As I was the principal photographer in the family and the self-designated "keeper of pictures," I would put a slideshow together that contained photographs from December first of the prior year through the end of November of the current year. We called the slideshow the *Luby Year in Review*. I included popular music from the year and we would watch it, as a family, on Christmas Eve. It was common for the slideshow to last an hour or more. It was always a great reminder of what we, individually and as a family, had done and experienced over the prior year. As I wouldn't let the family see it until Christmas Eve, there was always anticipation as to how many embarrassing pictures I had and which ones would make the *Luby Year in Review*.

So now the question was whether or not we wanted to be reminded of all that had happened in this last year. How could I put together a *Year in Review* and how would I treat Conner's death? Would it help us to move on or would it fan the pain of grief?

I worked particularly long and hard on this edition of the *Luby Year in Review*. I sensed that it was important, if for no reason other than that someday Moira would be able to show her children this slideshow and help to explain what it was like to lose her big brother. When Christmas Eve arrived, a small group of friends wanted to come by and view it. The slideshow contained every picture of Conner that I could find from December through September, even if I otherwise would not have included them. As I approached the date of the accident, I had the music fade out and then showed the photographs I had taken from the balcony of the Stephanie Inn showing the sun set over the ocean. These pictures had been taken the night before his accident. Jane and I had been drinking wine that beautiful summer evening, and I remember taking the pictures of the sun slowly sinking into the ocean. The music I selected for the transition from pre-accident to post-accident was "Smile," as sung by Lyle Lovett.

Smile though your heart is aching
Smile even though it's breaking
When there are clouds in the sky, you'll get by

If you smile through your fear and sorrow
Smile and maybe tomorrow
You'll see the sun come shining through for you

Light up your face with gladness
Hide every trace of sadness
Although a tear may be ever so near

That's the time you must keep on trying
Smile, what's the use of crying
You'll find that life is still worthwhile
If you just smile

That's the time you must keep on trying
Smile, what's the use of crying
You'll find that life is still worthwhile
If you just smile
© Charlie Chaplin

At the end of the slideshow, I knew that I needed to include a tribute to Conner. One of Conner's signature "looks" was of him smiling and giving a "thumbs up," using one or both hands. In looking back, I found that he had done this most of his life whenever he saw a camera pointed at him. I was able to find dozens and dozens of photographs with him giving the thumbs up. I also had pictures of friends and family also giving the thumbs up. Some had been taken in the past and others were done in the months after Conner's death.

In all subsequent *Luby Year in Reviews*, I've always found a way to sneak in a couple of pictures of Conner. It is important to do so to confirm that Conner remains part of us even if he isn't physically with us.

chapter twenty-two
dreams

I came into my dream sitting at a restaurant table by myself. The table was clear, and the fact that I was alone was clear, everything else was hazy and fuzzy as if I were in the middle of a fog. I began to hear people shouting and having a good time. I ignored the chaos, however, as I continued to feel alone, mourning the death of my little baby girl.

I remember looking down at the table where I was sitting, thinking about how different my life would be if I could just have Leilani back in my life. At that moment someone shouted my name. I looked toward my right and saw what appeared to be a heavy crowd having the time of their lives. All the bodies were in the distance, fuzzy and in a fog, much like my other surroundings. Suddenly, I saw a hand pop up in the crowd and frantically wave as if to gain my attention. I kept hearing "Hey!!! Gloria!!! Heeeey!"

As I stared hard into the crowd, Conner appeared and began running toward me.

He was the only other person or thing in the dream that was clear. He ran up to me and hugged me tight. I felt his warmth spread to me and it seemed to become more intense the longer it lasted. He hugged me and rocked me back and forth, saying "It's so great to see you Little One (which is the nickname he called me back in high school)."

I remember telling myself "Don't let go! Don't let go!" (Conner's hugs were always the BEST) and somehow my sorrow dissipated. I finally broke away from his hug to see if I were dreaming or if it truly was him. I looked into those beautiful blue eyes of his and, before I could say anything, Conner said, "Oh me? I'm doing great!" and he smiled that smile I remember so well.

I figured heaven was too large a place for him to have had encountered my daughter but the thought crossed my mind to ask. Once again, before I had the chance to say anything, Conner looked into my eyes and said, simply and softly, "She is doing fine."

The most amazing and intense warmth then filled my body as I knew that by "she," he meant my daughter. I understood that Conner was the one who would seek out the loved ones who've passed, checking in on them as he would check in on us.

I had no words, I began to cry in my dream for the comfort of knowing my baby was happy and safe. The comfort of missing my friend, but knowing he is always around, was more than overwhelming.

Conner's last words to me were "Gotta run! Party time!" which undeniably had Conner written all over it!

As I woke up I turned toward my husband who asked me "Did you sleep well?" and, of course, I answered "Better than ever"

-Marie Escamilla

Since his death, I have had two particularly strong dreams involving Conner. The first came to me the night of his death. In this dream, I was driving south on Interstate 5 and the accident site was on the other side of the median strip. I couldn't see the vehicles but I could see the flashing lights of the emergency vehicles. I had the sense that it was "the" accident site but wasn't quite ready to feel the emotions of knowing that it was Conner on the other side of the median.

All of a sudden, I saw sparks shooting up into the night sky. There was no immediate explanation for the sparks but they were beautiful. Unlike the reds and blues of the emergency vehicles' strobe lights, these were multicolored and shooting high into the sky. I awoke immediately after the dream ended and tried to figure out what it meant. Whether it was my vivid imagination or some sort of spiritual epiphany, I recognized that the sparks were Conner's spirit being released from his body.

There was no question in my mind that I had been given a glimpse of something special. For just a moment, an all-too-brief moment, the shock of Conner's death was replaced by a calm that was both warm and comforting. I knew that Conner was still out there—somewhere and somehow.

The second dream came to me a couple of weeks later. In that dream, I walked out of our bathroom to see Conner lying on our bed. He was shirtless and shoeless and wearing a pair of his ratty jeans. I looked at him and knew that he was dead. There wasn't any sadness or fear but, rather, just a feeling of objective observation. This was the body of my beautiful, recently deceased son and there was nothing unusual about the fact that his body was lying on my bed.

As I stood there staring at him, I noticed that his chest was moving, as if he was breathing. This, however, didn't strike me as unusual despite the fact that I knew he was dead. All of a sudden, he opened his eyes and sat up. I remained standing where I was, just observing all of this with a certain degree of detachment. It seemed real but unreal, all at the same time, and I felt no fear or unease. Slowly, Conner stood up and walked over to me. He opened his arms and then wrapped them around me— one of those "Conner hugs" that were so complete and unique. The hug was strong and warm and all-encompassing. I put my arms around him and, even now, would swear that I felt the skin of his back. His skin was warm and soft. It was a complete sensory experience. I could see him. I could feel him. The only thing I couldn't experience was hearing him. He was silent throughout the entire dream. And then it was over. It ended with the embrace and a feeling of innate love being exchanged.

When I awoke shortly thereafter, I still had the feeling of peace and calm that I had found in his embrace. I also had a measure of joy for the first time since the accident. I felt as if Conner had come back to show me that he loved me and that he always would. Maybe it was his way of saying goodbye to me. Maybe it was my way of finally accepting his death and saying goodbye to him. Whatever it was, I was grateful to have one last "Conner hug." It was the only dream I ever had like that, no matter how often I have hoped for another.

I have had other dreams in which Conner was present. Often they are dreams involving the whole family, and there isn't any conscious understanding that Conner has died. In other dreams, he is there but usually in the background. I know that he is dead but accept his presence in the dream without fear or regret. In none of the dreams have I ever heard his voice.

Jane has also had some dreams in which Conner was present, dreams from which she also gained immense and immediate comfort. Others, friends and family, have also had dreams of Conner. I have come to categorize dreams of Conner into two distinct types. The first is a "memory" dream. That is a dream where Conner is present but you don't know that he has passed. Even if it isn't a memory of a specific incident, it is a general memory of Conner and what he meant to the person dreaming. One of his best "gal pals" from grade school still has frequent dreams of Conner. In these dreams, they are kids again, traipsing through the back trails of Cook Park, just running and laughing, carefree and joyful. Unfortunately, in none of the dreams can she hear his voice and in none of these dreams can she feel him. They are memories of earlier times, more carefree and simpler, and Conner has come to epitomize those times for her.

The second type of dream is what I consider to be a "message" dream. In this type of dream Conner seems to be reaching out. The person is aware that Conner is dead but he is an active participant in the dream. He seems to be trying to contact the person and give some sort of message. My two dreams would qualify as message dreams.

Marie Escamilla's dream would also be considered a message dream.

What became frustrating about the message dreams is that the more you wanted one, the less likely you were to receive one. For months, and even years, Moira longed for a dream of Conner but, at most, she would sense his presence in dreams but couldn't see him. Finally, years after the accident, Moira had her first dream of Conner. In her dream, she was at a party and Conner was there. She knew that he was dead, so at first, she just thought it was someone who looked like him. She started to take pictures of this Conner look-alike with her phone because the resemblance was so amazing. She began to wonder if, in fact, it really was Conner. Her friend Rachel then walked up to her and asked what she was doing. Moira told her that she was "taking pictures of Conner." Rachel then told her that Conner wasn't there. When Moira looked down at the pictures on her phone, they were all of an elderly Asian man. She then just started crying as the dream faded and she woke up with the tears still streaming down her face.

I'm not sure if this was a message dream and, if it was, what possible message Conner could have been giving. Of course, knowing Conner's peculiar sense of humor, it is possible that he was just messing with his little sister. That would not have been an atypical thing for Conner Patrick Luby to do.

For others, the dreams never came—no matter how much they wanted them—or if they did, they arrived years later.

Megan McAninch longed to see Conner again. A little over four years after the accident, she finally had her message dream from Conner. In this dream, Megan was walking down Regent Street in London with a friend. They had just passed Hamleys Toy Shop when she heard Conner call her name. Before she could turn all the way around, he wrapped her up in a bear hug. She pushed him away so that she could look at him and then, with tears in her eyes, they hugged one another. She pulled back again to look at him and he said, "Finally! I've been trying to get to you for fucking ever!" The dream then ended and Megan woke up with tears in her eyes and a smile on her lips and whispered, "Thank you."

One person who perhaps had the most dreams involving Conner was an old friend from high school, Molly Jones. Molly is an interesting person. She and Conner were friends in high school but had a sudden falling–out during Conner's senior year. While they talked about their fight, they hadn't yet fully reconciled when he died. She somehow felt as if she had lost Conner's respect and didn't see any way to get it back.

When she first learned of Conner's death, Molly was plunged into a confusing swirl of shock, sadness, guilt, regret and, perhaps most frustrating and overwhelming of all, complete numbness. She couldn't cry. She had no idea of how to feel or to express what feelings she could identify. She refused to attend his memorial mass. It wasn't that she didn't care for him or that she didn't *want* to be there to honor him, but she felt that she didn't *deserve* to be there. She blamed herself for the schism in their relationship. She was consumed with a mixture of guilt and emptiness.

Nonetheless, it was Molly who had the most dreams of Conner. We have speculated that Conner found her an easier conduit than others to get his message out. He knew that Molly would share her dreams with those who needed him. (In writing this paragraph, I had a sense of Conner laughing at my suggestion that Molly might be "easier" than others.)

Molly's first dream came to her just weeks after the accident. She describes it as follows:

He was wearing a bright green shirt with that shaggy blonde California-boy hair of his and a very happy, peaceful look on his face. From the very moment I saw him, I knew I was dreaming. I was also distinctly aware that just because I was dreaming didn't mean it wasn't real.

I immediately ran over to my Mom. I remember explicitly saying to her, "MOM! CONNER IS HERE! I know, I know, this is just a dream, but this is the only way I will be able to talk to him, so I'm going to."

I have to interject here that I have never experienced this type of awareness in a dream before or since. It wasn't like a regular lucid dream in which you know you're dreaming and have control over everything that happens. I was fully aware of my state of mind and why it was taking place that way. It felt exactly like real life but it was just happening in a place where Conner and I could again both see each other.

My Mom responded simply, "Well, go talk to him then!" So I did. I ran over to him and spilled out everything I had been feeling and all the things I wished I could have said. I told him how sorry I was that our friendship ended, that I blamed myself for it, and that I wished we could have fixed it. I told him how guilty I felt and that I didn't know if I was supposed to be sad. I think I even told him I was afraid to go to his funeral. I just kept repeating over and over how sorry I was.

Finally, he stopped me. I looked into his face and saw an expression I can't really explain. I'm not sure I ever saw it on his face in real life. He looked so happy, so whole, and so at peace with absolutely everything.

"Molly," he said gently. "It's okay. I know." Then he just gave me a huge Conner hug. I knew then that he had forgiven me—that, regardless of whether or not he really had forgiven me before he died, he was now in a place where things like that no longer mattered. He seemed very self-assured and complete, like nothing good could be missing from his life and everything bad had been shed away.

The terrible thoughts that had been eating me alive, and all the things I couldn't let go of, were simply no longer important. He had let them go and forgiven me. I knew I could now to start to forgive myself.

That day was the first day I was able to cry, and I cried a lot. It was as though I had been holding back an explosion. I felt like I finally had his permission to grieve however I needed to.

Over the following years, Molly would continue to have dreams but none as real or complete as that first dream. Some of them were just visits where Conner popped up on a random basis and, in others, it felt to her as if he was trying to tell her something. He had a way of coming to her when she was upset. One time, after crying herself to sleep over a guy, she had a dream of Conner leading a cha-cha line. He was smiling and laughing as he extended the cha-cha line to her shoulders.

In other dreams, she had conversations with him. Molly explains one of these dreams as follows:

*He and I were just hanging out and it was basically one giant lovefest—
we talked about everything: high school, why we were friends, etc. I think
I cried a lot telling him how much I missed him, but for the most part I
was happy. We even cuddled. He kept saying he was "breaking the rules"
by being there, but that he didn't care.*

*This was the first time I wasn't one of the only few people who could see
him—I was just one of the only people who recognized him. I pointed him
out to one guy and said, "Do you know who this is?"*

*The guy freaked out and was like, "Conner Luby! But he died a year
ago!" That was "breaking the rules," so Conner disappeared for a while.*

*Then we were stunting—me flying, Megan Mac backing, and a whole
bunch of girls who had never stunted before dropping me on top of her over
and over. She got hit really hard in the head and then Conner reappeared
behind her right shoulder and started spotting. He and Megan Mac then
had a moment, and I let them do their thing.*

*Then I started talking to Conner again and he decided that he needed
to be in disguise with long black hair and glasses. We had a sort of Tom
Sawyer moment—it was even in a church like the one in the movie where
Tom listened to his own funeral. It was some kind of memorial service for
Conner and he was attending in disguise. There was this man who didn't
recognize him and gave him a very solemn lecture about letting this be a
lesson to him, that he should never waste his youth because you never know
how much time you have left. We tried not to laugh.*

*Later I asked him what it was like to be dead and he said, "Have you
ever passed out?"*

*I said, "I think so, but I don't remember anything from it—I don't
think you are conscious or dream at all."*

He said, "You have to make yourself."

One of Conner's oldest friends, Jonathan Pelzner, had a beautiful
dream of Conner only weeks after he died. Jon recounted the dream as
follows:

I was driving in a car and Conner was in the passenger seat. I don't remember whose car it was, or even who was driving, but I know that we were going to pick up Jason and I was sitting right behind Conner. We were talking about how Conner had passed away and Conner was, like, "Yeah, I'm just doing my thing and waiting to get in. I'm really excited about it. It's going to be really sweet." He then said something about there being a bunch of girls up there that he would be able to hook up with.

Somehow I started to talk about this girl I know; her name is Courtney. He had never met her but, in my dream, he knew her. He said, "Yeah, man, I could get her!"

I responded, "No, you couldn't."

He then just got that sly grin of his and said, "Yeah, I could get her."

After going back and forth like this for a while, I said, "Conner, it doesn't matter if you could or couldn't get her. You can't because, well, you're dead. It's not going to happen. She's mine."

He then just looked down and quietly said "Oh."

At that point, we picked up Jason and started driving again. We parked in a gravel parking lot and, to the left, was a line of trees and an embankment down to a nice big lake. We all got out of the car. It was Conner, Jeff, Jason, and me. We walked around to the back of the car and opened the trunk. Inside was all of Conner's stuff. This was stuff that meant something to him – his gold Top-siders, his old poncho, and a bunch of other stuff. We were all "claiming" them and Conner was standing there laughing. He was helping to dole his stuff out to the four of us. Suddenly he turned around and walked off toward the lake.

The rest of us were standing there, watching him and wondering what was going on. We watched him for what seemed like minutes as he just stood on top of the embankment looking out at the lake. I walked up beside him and stood next to him. Not a single word was said between us. I just continued to look at him as he gazed out over the lake. After a couple of more minutes, we walked back to the car and all just drove off. No more words were said.

chapter twenty-three
... and then what?

Conner was the first friend I had at Jesuit. On our very first day of Freshman year, Conner sat next to me. He instantly struck up a conversation: Where was I from? What did I like to do? Did I have any good-looking friends? We were asked repeatedly by the teacher to be quiet.

The next year we had physics together. Giving the class free rein to sit where they pleased was a mistake on the part of Doctor Moloseau because Conner and I, now along with Kevin McShane, were already pros at being disruptive goofballs. I remember how regularly we would sneak to the back of the class and watch the first big viral hit, "The End of The World."

My fondest high school memories always involve Conner. He could make you smile no matter how bad the day; no matter how sad the moment; and no matter how inappropriate the timing.

-Ashley Kennelly Ullman
née Kendig

So then what? What happens next? Is the wound still healing or is it now healed? Does the wound ever heal? Does the scar fade over time? In a perfect world, that is exactly what would happen. The grief would fade and you would be left with nothing but wonderful memories of a great child. Of course, in a perfect world, Conner would not be dead. So no, the wound never completely heals and the scar never entirely fades.

As a parent, I am caught between two very contrasting emotions.

The first is the desire to heal, the need to live and laugh, the longing for a return to better and happier times. I have a primal urge to feel the same sense of carefree happiness that I remember experiencing in the past. I understand, however, that the only way to do that is to block out the pain, and the only way to truly block out the pain is to block out the memory of Conner, or at least the memory of his death. I just can't do that; I can't forget any part of my son, his life and his death and so, the pain remains. When I find myself laughing and being happy, a nagging guilt often makes me question what right I have to be joyful without Conner. What kind of father could do that? It is a never-ending conflict of emotions.

I remember feeling guilty the first time that Jane and I made love after Conner died. It was only a few weeks after the accident. More than ever, Jane and I loved and needed each other but I was torn all the while, thinking about whether it was appropriate to experience pleasure again. I could not get Conner out of my mind, nor the constant realization that I would never see him again. The lovemaking was as joyless as it was necessary. It was our first step in re-establishing our lives—a small step perhaps—but a very important step.

The rational part of my brain understands that joy and grief are not mutually exclusive. I understand that I can be happy despite the fact that my son is dead but that doesn't stop the guilt. The guilt is that I am somehow betraying my child. Was he so unimportant to me that life can go on, that I can be happy again? It is as if I am having a picnic in a beautiful park with Jane and Moira but I can't stop focusing on those rain clouds in the distance. The happiness is never complete and care-free. The dark clouds of grief are never far away. Over the ensuing years, as those dark clouds became less noticeable, the guilt only increased.

It may seem a bit masochistic, but you really don't want the guilt and the grief to go away. The pain of grief is a reminder of the love you felt, and still feel, for your child. If there can be no true loss without love, than there can be no loss without real pain.

I know that I desperately want to retain that same feeling of love for Conner that I felt when he was alive. Unfortunately, that feeling has started to ebb as the years pass and as new memories of life without Conner replace those of life with him. I forget what his voice sounds like. I forget what he smells like. I forget his laugh and I know that the photographs never really captured the enormity of his smile. The pain of grief is welcome as it triggers those memories of life with Conner and results in a wonderful pastiche of both joy and pain.

* * *

In the years following the accident, Conner's death triggered unexpected situations. One of the most common occurrences arises when meeting new people. Invariably, as we try and get each other's background stories, the question always comes up: "So, how many kids do you have?"

What is the answer to that question? The simple, but incomplete, answer is two but that raises the question of whether Jane and I still have two children, or is it more accurate to say we *had* two children. Using the present tense just invites follow-up questions like how old they are or whether they are still in school. Using the past tense leads to the uncomfortable question of what happened. No one wants to discuss the death of a child, and certainly not with someone new. This is as uncomfortable for us as it is for the people we've just met. .

Jane and I struggled long and hard with this. Saying that we only have one child seemed to us to be a betrayal of Conner. It made us feel guilty, as if we were denying his existence. We tried to not mention Conner to casual acquaintances or gave vague responses to this initial inquiry, but that turned a simple conversation into a walk through a minefield. We spent so much time dodging the issue that we sometimes appeared evasive and guarded, which could be off-putting to others.

Over time, we developed certain methods to "slip" the question. When asked how many children we have, we just say that we have a daughter who is off at college. This seems to be a good blend of truth and misdirection and is in no way a betrayal of Conner. Generally, this response solves the problem and, at most, leads to follow-up questions about where she is going to school and how old she is.

Occasionally, however, it is not enough. Occasionally, someone will ask the follow-up question, "So, you only have just the one child?"

This question always amazes me and still sometimes angers me. What kind of question is that? What answer are you really looking for? Are you trying to figure out if this person that you just met is hiding some deep, dark secret about their children? Do you think that our lives are somehow less fulfilled, if in fact, we only have just the one child? Are we lesser persons and/or parents than you if, in fact, we only have just the one child?

The first couple of times this happened, I responded, "No, we had a son but he died in a car accident." I would then just stare at the person and watch them cast their eyes downward in an awkward attempt to avoid the topic. I would know, right then and there, that this was a relationship that had no future. I know that this was an immature response to an insensitive question, but I still experienced a measure of satisfaction in causing the discomfort. In hindsight, it was likely caused by my grief and anger seeping through the cracks. Over time I began to understand that this follow-up question wasn't intended to seek out any deep, dark family secret. Rather, it was simply meant to continue a conversation and to create an opening for people to tell us about their children. Over time I learned how to respond to this question so as to acknowledge Conner, but to at least keep the possibility alive of building a new friendship. I still slip up from time to time but it all depends upon my mood and my first impression of this person I have just met. The more I like a person, the harder I try to ease any potential discomfort.

The thing is that Jane and I both want to talk about Conner. We enjoy talking about Conner. Rather than being painful or uncomfortable, it is actually refreshing to be able to talk about him. It reminds us that Conner was here and that people remember him. It reminds us that he had an impact upon people that far exceeded ordinary expectations of someone who had not even reached his twenty-first birthday. He was such an important part of our lives, and we have so many wonderful memories of him, that we relish the opportunity to talk about him.

While it happens to Jane more than it does me, we still run into people from time to time who knew Conner. Jane might be at the grocery store or getting a pedicure, and someone will see the name on her debit card. They will say something like, "Luby? Are you Conner's Mom?" This always makes us happy to know that people remember Conner; that people want to tell us what they remember about him.

Unfortunately, there are far too few friends who feel comfortable talking about Conner these days, and far too few strangers we meet who knew him. Some former friends still avoid us and for them, the die is cast. It is too late to bridge that gulf. They will forever and for always be former friends, just something else lost in that fiery crash of September 12, 2009.

Despite the loss of some friends, new friends have come into our lives. Two of our now closest friends didn't know Conner personally at all. They were former clients of mine with a daughter in Conner's class and another in Moira's class. We saw them at Jesuit functions but it was more a casual relationship than a friendship.

About a year after Conner's death, they invited us to have some wine at their house. They were reaching out to us out of a sense of compassion. One glass of wine turned into three or four and, before we knew it, it was well past midnight and we were still talking. We talked about Conner and about our sense of loss and grief. We talked about Conner and the impact his life and death had on their children. It was wonderful to speak with friends about Conner without any uneasiness. They have become a bright beam of light allowing us to celebrate a wondrous life while also acknowledging a tragic death.

* * *

So what happens next? I can't help but wonder which of us dies next. Now that death has visited our family once, it is obvious that further visits are coming. I hate this thought but can't banish it from my mind. Jane and I are both moving into our late fifties and the odds are that one of us will die next. I fear that it might be me. This isn't a fear *for* me because, as I've said before, I see death as an adventure. My fear is for Jane and Moira.

Moira is well on her way to having a very successful life, and Jane and I have learned how to save for the future. No, my fear isn't based on the financial repercussions of my death but, rather, the emotional and psychological impact. Jane and I have been together for so long and our lives are so intertwined that I question how she would cope with my death. Even more so, I fear the effect upon Moira. While she is strong, she does not yet have the support network in place to assist her with my passing. Jane would do her best to provide emotional support for Moira but I don't know what truly would happen to Moira. I don't know what my death would do to her psychologically and I fear that—a lot.

If Jane dies first, and this is something that I have contemplated, my life would be much the worse but I would survive. A large part of who I am and what I am would die with her. Nonetheless, I would force myself to survive because of Moira. She and I have such a special relationship and are so similar in so many ways that we could, and would, help each other deal with that loss.

Of course, there is the hope that Jane and I live for another twenty years or more. We dream of the opportunity to play with our future grandchildren. We imagine ourselves as the doting grandparents. Our hope is that, when the time comes, we die peacefully and gracefully. Our hope is that Moira will have the support of her husband and children to help her with her grieving.

Shortly before my father died, I was able to fly down to San Diego and introduce him to Moira, his last grandchild. She was only six months old at the time and, of course, has no memory of him. As we were leaving, I realized that it was unlikely that I would ever see him alive again. He was fighting a losing battle with various forms of cancer and the end was rapidly approaching. We all knew it.

When it was time to leave, and with Moira down in the car with my mother, I had the opportunity to say goodbye to my father. I hugged him, and with tears streaming down my face, told him that he was a good father. I felt that it was important that he know that, despite any disagreements and disapprovals in the past, I loved him. He looked at me and told me that I was a good son. We then kissed one another and I turned and left. I never saw him again but was comforted that I was able to say goodbye to him and know that he understood.

My mother's demise was more gradual. She gradually lost the ability to engage in substantive conversation and suffered from short-term memory loss, interspersed with occasional bouts of delusion. On occasion, she vented racist comments and made violent threats, nothing we had ever heard from her before. Eventually my siblings and I placed her in a nursing home and she promptly shut down, both mentally and physically. By the time she died, I was reconciled to the fact that this woman was no longer my mother. There was no saying goodbye to this shell of a woman who was not the mother that had raised me and whom I had loved my whole life. That woman was already gone and what remained was merely the odious husk of my mother.

I'm hopeful that Jane's and my passing will be more akin to my father's than my mother's. We want to be able to comfort Moira as we pass away. This is the last thing that we, as parents, want to be able to do for her. We want her to be able to become accustomed to the concept of our passing rather than having it thrust upon her, suddenly and without any forewarning. Conner's death did that to her and we don't want her to have to go through that again. This is what we hope for but we also know that we have little, if any, say in what will actually happen.

I can only hope that Moira will be old enough, and have a strong enough support system in place, to be able to cope when the time comes. She's had more than her share of grief and deserves better. It frustrates me to know that I can't ensure that; that I can't protect her from any more pain.

All I can do is to let Moira know, each and every day, that I love

her. I make a point, now more than ever, to let her know what a wonderful daughter she is. I send her random texts that say, "I love my girl!"
I want her to be able to look back and know that she had a wonderful
childhood, even if it has to be qualified by the phrase, "all things considered." I want her to know, forever and for always, that she is loved.

* * *

In the years following Conner's death, I thought that I had become inured to the pain of a child's death. After all, I had survived and, as the
saying goes, whatever doesn't kill you, makes you stronger. I read about
tragedies in the newspaper and sympathized with the grieving parents
from a distance. I sent my letters of condolence. I offered to meet with
the newest members of the "Club" and was honestly disappointed when
my offers were rarely accepted.

I was stronger than others because of what I had experienced. Then
I received the telephone call that Trevor Sullivan had died. Trevor was
Conner's age. His mom had worked for me several years before. I knew
his mom and dad well, as well his siblings.

A mutual friend had called to tell me that Travis died in a motorcycle accident in Los Angeles. I was stunned but, with my newfound
strength, sprang into action. I placed calls to people who needed to
know and then drove to Trevor's parents' house. As I pulled up, I could
see that the house was quiet, with only a couple of people milling about.
I parked my car in the street, stood up and then realized I was nervous.
All of a sudden, I didn't know what to say. I had no idea how to offer my
condolences and compassion to a real person, face-to-face.

I willed myself to walk up the driveway, trying to rehearse lines that
all sounded stilted and insincere. As I approached the house, Trevor's
mom came out to greet me. All I could do was hug her and say "Pam,
I am so sorry."

Conscious of avoiding the "pity" look, I tried to make small talk
and failed miserably. Trevor's dad came out and we tried to talk, but it

was clear that I was not necessarily a welcome presence. Jane came by and we tried to share our experience but that was the wrong thing to do. This wasn't about us showing them the way to grieve. This wasn't about us and having "been there; done that." This was about *them* grieving and finding their own way. We wanted to help but our presence seemed to make their experience tougher for all of us.

We dropped by several times over the following days and tried to bring levity to the situation by talking about Trevor and encouraging others to also do so. This was *our* way of dealing with our grief, but it turned out that it was not *their* way of dealing with *their* grief. It was a difficult and humbling lesson to realize that I didn't know it all. I realized that I had failed them.

While my experience with Trevor's death was difficult, it was a situation where I knew Trevor's parents much better than I had known him. I knew that he was a great kid and shared many of the same attributes as Conner but I didn't really know him. My grief was more for his parents and siblings than for him.

Things were different when I heard about Seabrooke.

* * *

When Jane first became an orthodontic assistant back in the mid-1980s, she worked with a young woman named Leslie Mooney and they became friends. Leslie was quirky and relatively unsophisticated but she had a good heart. When her daughter Seabrooke was born, we cheered for her. When she divorced her husband and eventually remarried, we became close friends with her and her new husband.

We socialized together and our kids got to know one another very well. Leslie and her husband Ron, together with Seabrooke, often came for visits and spent some holidays with us. I enjoyed watching Seabrooke grow from being a very sheltered and naïve young girl into a vibrant and adventurous young woman. After high school, Seabrooke recognized that she needed to leave Oregon in order to grow, so she moved to Denver. She put herself through the University of Colorado and explored her artistic talents through painting, photography and film.

We kept in touch and she often credited me with encouraging her to challenge and explore her religious beliefs. She truly became one of my favorite young people even though I rarely got to see her once she moved to Colorado.

Then on a Wednesday, I received a text message from her stepfather that said, "Can we come see you. Seabrooke is missing." I dropped everything and called him immediately. He explained that Seabrooke had gone to Argentina on a backpacking trip hoping to find an organic farm to work on for a while. They had just received a call from the US Embassy telling them that she had been involved in a serious bus crash the previous Friday and that they didn't know where she was.

While waiting for them to come by, I got online and researched bus crashes in Argentina. I read that a truck had been stolen and that the intoxicated driver had run headfirst into the oncoming bus. Seventeen of the thirty-five people on board were killed either by the impact or the fireball that had then erupted. My stomach was in knots.

When Leslie and Ron arrived at my office, they were numb and tried to fill me in on some additional, yet still sketchy, information. The Embassy advised them that a passerby had provided some first aid to an American who was able to say that her last name was Mooney. The passerby had observed Seabrooke being taken away in an ambulance. No one knew at that point what hospital she had been taken to or what her condition was.

Leslie and Ron needed to get some information to the Embassy so that they could speak with us. I aided them in shipping the necessary documents to Buenos Aires.

The next morning we heard from the Embassy. They had located Seabrooke's remains. My heart sank at the news.

For the first time, I was actively mourning for someone other than Conner—not just sharing grief with parents. I was grieving for Seabrooke. I didn't think that the death of a young person could affect me like this again, but I was wrong. While it ripped the scab off my grief for Conner, it was a new grief. This was a grief for Seabrooke. It might not have been as powerful as it was with Conner, but it was strong and it hurt.

Now I had to realize that rather than strengthening me against the ravages of grief, Conner's death had actually made me more sensitive to it.

* * *

Conner died six weeks before his twenty-first birthday. With Moira's twenty-first birthday approaching, I calculated, to the day, when she would pass her brother—when she would officially be older than Conner. That day was August 20, 2013. From that day forward, she would forever after be older than her brother.

I debated with myself as to whether to share this calculation with Jane and Moira. Jane and I had discussed how difficult it would be for Moira when she turned twenty-one, to know that she was older than Conner. We had, however, never discussed the August 20 date.

I finally decided not to tell either of them. Neither of them needed another reminder of how Conner's life had been cut short. I would know and I would silently acknowledge this life event alone.

When the day finally arrived, we were surprised by a call from Moira telling us the significance of the day. We toasted the day with a shot of Irish whiskey, knowing that Conner would have approved of that.

Jane was surprised by this event; I was not. Deep in my heart, I was proud of Moira and the fact that she was so much like me.

* * *

So, again, now what? What happens next? There are no set answers to those questions. More than ever before, I realize how impermanent and fragile life is. Prior to September 12, 2009, I tended to live in the future. While Jane and I would make yearly goals each New Year's Eve, my eye was often fixed on the far future. I would imagine what our lives would be like in three years or five years or more. I would imagine walking Moira down the aisle, and holding Conner's first child in my arms. The world was mine for the taking and I was golden.

Friends have passed in and out of our lives. Some came because of Conner and others because of Moira. Most of the "brothers" have moved on and Moira has lost touch with most of the friends who provided her support in those early days. We are all so different than we were. Some of the changes have been for the better and many others for the worse.

Life has changed drastically in these few short years. I've learned to focus on the here and now. My plans are usually measured in months rather than years. I take greater care with my relationship with Jane and Moira. I've learned to enjoy the simple pleasure of a setting sun or a warm breeze. I'm no longer as materialistic as I once was. Things that I once coveted are now merely things. I focus on experiences more than just accumulating more "stuff."

And I've found that the pain has lessened. Without realizing it, I've noticed that I no longer feel a void in my being. Whether I want it to happen or not, Conner is starting to fade into the past. He is still my son and will always be so but he's not here. He wasn't here last Christmas or the Christmas before that, or the one before that. He wasn't here on Moira's last birthday or the birthday before that.

We keep him a presence in our lives by toasting him with Irish whiskey on birthdays and anniversaries. We try and honor him by taking his ashes with us when we travel and spreading them in places that he would have wanted to visit. We still make sure that he "gives" birthday and Christmas gifts to each of us – all wrapped in tinfoil. We wonder what he would be doing if he were still alive and speculate on what his achievements would have been.

We do all this without the same feeling of loss as before. The wound has, much to our surprise, substantially healed and scarred over. The times are much fewer and far between when I go dark and peer over the ledge into the abyss. I wear my scar with pride. I am not the father who has lost a child but, rather, the father of two wonderful children.

I still feel guilt about Conner's diminishing role in our lives, but it is a guilt that I have adjusted to. The question of whether the guilt has lessened in intensity, or if I have just become better able to absorb it, is one that I can't answer.

Perhaps most importantly, I continue to strive to become a better person. It is important that I become the person that Conner would have been proud of, not just when he was a child, but if he had become a man. I recognize that I am still flawed but know that I can be better. I will be better. Perhaps most importantly, I now strive to become the man that Moira will be proud of…for the rest of her life.

chapter twenty-four
crashing waves

We're driving in my Dad's convertible, top down, 78 degrees and sunshiny. It's just us and nothing but smiles and laughter and sunglasses and wind and music and singing and hands and hair blowing everywhere. We come over the Coast Range as the sun starts setting; it's a race to the horizon to make it for the Green Flash. We're racing with the music, trying to pause time, thinking that maybe if we hold our breath, if we breathe just a little slower, time might slow down with us.

We tear through the parking lot. We stumble down the dunes and, out-of-breath, collapse into the sand just before the last bit of fire kisses the ocean goodnight.

We blink…and we miss it.

-Megan McAninch

As every parent knows, you willingly make sacrifices for your children but you also have an obligation to your spouse to keep the marriage alive and strong. Jane and I were getting ready to celebrate our twenty-fifth wedding anniversary.

With Conner planning on going to Africa in January and then possibly to join the military, and with Moira still at Jesuit, a weekend getaway at the Stephanie Inn in Cannon Beach seemed to be our best choice. It would give us some alone time but we wouldn't be too far away. We were supposed to leave early on that Friday afternoon but, as always seemed to happen, problems arose. I had been in court most of the day and the hearing ran long. I called Jane at about 2:30 p.m. as I was leaving the courthouse on my way back to the office to drop off some files. She was not happy.

In addition to the fact that I was late and the incredibly beautiful afternoon was only getting later, Moira had come down with a bug. Jane suggested that we just cancel our getaway. I told her that we could talk about it when I got home and then promptly dropped my briefcase off at the office and raced home.

As I was driving home, I received a call from Conner. "Dad," he said, "I know that Mom is pretty upset but you two really need to get away for the weekend."

I told him that while I appreciated his opinion, it was getting late and Moira wasn't feeling well. In addition, I told him that by leaving so late, we would run into all of the heavy traffic to the Coast. He then told me, "Dad, I'll take care of Moira. Mom really needs to get away." I agreed. He told me that he had already left the house but would be back later to take care of Moira.

By the time I got home, it took me only minutes to change and, as Jane had done most of my packing, we loaded up her car, kissed Moira goodbye, and took off. I am still not quite sure why we decided to take Jane's car rather than mine. It would have made more sense to take my car since it was a convertible and we were headed for a sunny weekend at the Coast. For whatever reason, we took Jane's car, thereby leaving the Saab at home.

The drive itself was uneventful, as we tried to decide if we wanted to golf the next day or just wander the Coast and explore the various small towns. We made good time and checked into the Stephanie Inn well before dinnertime. The Stephanie Inn is a lovely inn located just south of Cannon Beach and overlooking the beach. The room was gorgeous with a beautiful view of the setting sun over the ocean. As we were settling in, we called home to let the kids know that we had made it safely and to check in and see how Moira was feeling. Moira picked up the phone and she was crying. She explained that she felt like crap and that Conner hadn't come home yet. I calmed her down and told her that I would call Conner and have him come home and take care of her.

I know that I was throwing a bit of a pity party but I felt like crap. The weather was beautiful, it was a Friday evening, and I felt horrible. It was a combination of headache, upset stomach, scratchy throat, and general achiness. I was sixteen years old and still wanted someone to baby me while I was sick. I certainly didn't want to be stuck home alone on a Friday night.

I called Conner and mentally prepared myself for an argument about him having to "babysit" his sister. He answered his telephone and told me that he was at a friend's house in West Linn. With a disapproving tone, I told him that I needed him to go home and take care of his little sister. To my surprise, he said, "okay."

I explained that he didn't need to stay home all night but we wanted him home at least until Moira fell asleep. He, again, said, "Okay. I'll go home right now." There was no sarcasm or sense that he felt put out. I didn't get the impression that he was just telling me what I wanted to hear. Rather, he knew what he had to do and expressed no reluctance or hesitation in doing it. I was relieved. It was one more sign to us that he really was maturing into a responsible young man. He knew that with his parents out of town for a twenty-fifth wedding anniversary celebration, his little sister became his responsibility.

After talking to Mom and Dad, I felt better knowing that Conner was coming home. When he did get home, he ran up the stairs and brought me some popsicles. He had stopped at the grocery store on the way home and got them for me. It made me happy.

With everything settled on the home front, Jane and I sat out on the balcony and enjoyed a bottle of Pinot Noir. We talked about the future, both immediate- and long-term. We talked about how we had been so incredibly fortunate over the past twenty-five years and wondered what the next twenty-five years would be like.

I was upstairs in Mom and Dad's bed watching television and Conner was either downstairs or in his room, I don't remember. About the time I was starting to fall asleep, Conner popped his head in the door and asked if it was all right if he went back to the party.

As I was already half-asleep, I said, "Sure."

He ran down the stairs and I heard him say, "Love you, Sis!"

After dinner, Jane and I went to bed. We left the sliding door slightly ajar so that we could hear the waves crashing on the shore. The night air was cool but we spooned with my arms around Jane to keep her warm and safe as we settled into a peaceful slumber.

I remember waking up at some point in the night when Sophie started barking. I'd like to think that it was about the time of the accident but I can't really say for sure. I remember yelling out to Conner to let the dog out to pee. When he didn't answer, I thought to myself, Well, you're going to be responsible for cleaning up after the dog! I then fell back asleep.

Jane woke up in the middle of the night, which was unusual for her. She is generally a sound sleeper but that night she woke up for no apparent reason. It was dark and she could hear the waves outside our room. It took a moment for her to realize where she was. Unsure why she woke up or why she had a feeling of uneasiness, she fell back to sleep.

It was about 8:00 in the morning when I heard a knocking on the front door. I assume that whoever it was had tried the doorbell first but I was in such a deep sleep that I hadn't heard it. I yelled for Conner to go answer the door but, of course, there was no response.
I threw some clothes on, knowing that I both looked and felt like hell, and

went down the stairs, all the while muttering under my breath. I opened the door and there was a tall man there, with two state troopers standing behind him.

The man asked if my parents were home and I told him no. He then asked who owned a Saab convertible. I told him that it was my Dad's car but that he was at the beach and my brother had it.

Quite frankly, at that point I thought Conner had done something stupid like getting arrested or that they were looking for him for eluding the police. He had never done anything like that before, but with the police there, I just assumed that was the worst-case scenario.

The man then asked if Conner had any tattoos and I told him that he had four stars on the right side of his chest.

Jane and I woke up and it was a perfect morning. The sun was shining and it was warm without being hot. There was a light breeze and the ocean looked calm. We jumped in the shower and got ready to head out to breakfast and then to explore the Coast and maybe play some golf.

The man told me that he had some bad news—that my brother was dead. He told me to call my parents right away. I reached for the phone and called.

Just before we headed out the door, my phone rang. I saw that it was the home number, and knowing that it would be much too early for Conner to be up and calling, I answered it by saying "Good morning, Girly Girl, and how are you this glorious day?"

Daddy...

about the author

Kevin W. Luby is a lot of things and has done a lot in his life. What is important about him, however, is that he is a husband and a father. Everything else is irrelevant.

Made in the USA
San Bernardino, CA
18 September 2014